LEIBNIZ
AN INTRODUCTION

LEIBNIZ
An Introduction

C. D. BROAD

Edited by C. Lewy

CAMBRIDGE UNIVERSITY PRESS

Cambridge
London   New York   Melbourne

Published by the Syndics of the Cambridge University Press
The Pitt Building, Trumpington Street, Cambridge CB2 1RP
Bentley House, 200 Euston Road, London NW1 2DB
32 East 57th Street, New York, NY10022, USA
296 Beaconsfield Parade, Middle Park, Melbourne 3206, Australia

Library of Congress Catalogue Card Number: 74–31784

ISBN 0 521 20691 X hard covers
ISBN 0 521 09925 0 paperback

First published 1975
Reprinted with corrections 1979
First printed in Great Britain by
Western Printing Services Ltd., Bristol
Reprinted in Great Britain by BKT

CONTENTS

EDITOR'S PREFACE

C. D. Broad expressed a wish that after his death I should go through his unpublished writings and consider the possibility of preparing some of them for publication.

The present volume contains his Cambridge lectures on the Philosophy of Leibniz. Broad had lectured on Leibniz before, but the course in its present form was first given in the academic year 1948–9 and repeated, with some revisions, in 1949–50. Broad always wrote out his lectures fully beforehand, and the MS. on Leibniz is in a very good state. But his handwriting is small and close and in places very difficult to decipher. It is probably too much to hope that no words have been misread.

I have tried to reproduce the text so far as possible as it is in the MS. But I have expanded Broad's abbreviations of names and other words, and have introduced greater uniformity in spelling, punctuation, and the use of italics, quotation marks and capital letters.

Broad's system of references was, however, inadequate: with very few exceptions he gave no page references to the passages which he was quoting or discussing. I have therefore undertaken the labour of supplying those references. So far as the original texts are concerned I generally refer to Gerhardt's *Die Philosophischen Schriften von G. W. Leibniz*. In addition, I have tried to provide, whenever possible, a reference to a currently available English translation. As a rule I refer to Loemker's *G. W. Leibniz: Philosophical Papers and Letters* (2nd edition) which contains the fullest selection of Leibniz's work available in English. In a few places I also mention other translations when these are fuller or are of special interest. And of course I refer to other translations when the texts which are discussed do not occur in Loemker.

The task of providing those references was not always easy. In particular, it was sometimes difficult to locate a passage which Broad was only mentioning or paraphrasing. As a result the references may involve some errors; but I hope that most of them are correct.

I am very grateful to my friend and colleague Dr Ian Hacking for helping me to provide some of those references.

I have also appended a short Bibliographical Note expanding the references in Broad's list of Leibniz's main works.

Round brackets are Broad's; my own insertions are enclosed in square brackets.

Some of the material included in the work was published in the form of two articles in *Theoria* (vol. 12 (1946) and vol. 15 (1949)). I am grateful to the Editor for permission to reproduce it here.

C. LEWY

Trinity College, Cambridge
June 1974

In the present reprint I have corrected a number of misprints and misreadings. For some of these corrections I am indebted to Mr. J. R. Bambrough, Professor P. T. Geach and Dr. R. S. Woolhouse.

C.L.

February 1979

ABBREVIATIONS

G.

Die Philosophischen Schriften von Gottfried Wilhelm Leibniz, herausgegeben von C. I. Gerhardt, 7 vols. (Berlin, 1875–90).

G. M.

Leibnizens Mathematische Schriften, herausgegeben von C. I. Gerhardt, 7 vols. (Berlin and Halle, 1849–63).

Alexander

The Leibniz–Clarke Correspondence Together with Extracts from Newton's 'Principia' and 'Opticks', edited with an introduction and notes by H. G. Alexander (Manchester, 1956).

Couturat

Opuscules et fragments inédits de Leibniz. Extraits des manuscrits de la Bibliothèque royale de Hanovre, par Louis Couturat (Paris, 1903).

Langley

New Essays Concerning Human Understanding by Gottfried Wilhelm Leibniz Together with an Appendix Consisting of Some of His Shorter Pieces, translated by Alfred Gideon Langley (New York and London, 1896).

Loemker

Gottfried Wilhelm Leibniz: Philosophical Papers and Letters, a selection translated and edited with an introduction by Leroy E. Loemker (2nd edition, Dordrecht, 1969).

Mason

The Leibniz–Arnauld Correspondence, edited and translated by H. T. Mason with an introduction by G. H. R. Parkinson (Manchester, 1967).

Morris and Parkinson

Leibniz: Philosophical Writings, edited by G. H. R. Parkinson, translated by Mary Morris and G. H. R. Parkinson (London, 1973).

Russell

Bertrand Russell, *A Critical Exposition of the Philosophy of Leibniz with an Appendix of Leading Passages* (Cambridge, 1900).

1
LIFE AND WORKS

1 Life

Leibniz was born on 21 January 1646 at Leipzig, where his father was a lawyer and professor of philosophy. He started his career as a scholar very early. He went to the university at the age of fifteen, and before that he was interested in logic. While at the university he read Bacon's *De Augmentis*. He meant to be a lawyer, and in 1663 he went for a year to Jena to study law. Here his mathematical interests were first strongly stimulated.

In 1666 he submitted a legal thesis for a doctor's degree at the University of Leipzig. The degree was not granted, probably because Leibniz was only twenty at the time. But it was accepted by the University of Altdorf, which invited him to become a professor there. He refused the offer and went to Nürnberg, where he stayed for a year. While there he studied alchemy and magic, and is said to have been initiated into the Rosicrucians and made secretary of the local branch of the society.

In 1667 he entered the services of the Elector of Mainz, where he remained till 1672. During this time most of his published writings were political. His political writings were mostly against the ambitious designs of the French. Louis XIV was threatening Germany, and Leibniz formed a plan for diverting his ambition to the more Christian object of expelling the Turks from Egypt. He went to Paris in 1672 to explain this plan to Louis in person but, like most of Leibniz's diplomatic schemes, it came to naught. Leibniz laboured all his life to reconcile the Romanists and the Protestants in Germany, and also the Lutherans and the Calvinists. His great object was to get both religious and political peace, but he failed. He attached great importance to the existence of learned societies; he founded the Academy of Berlin, and was consulted about the foundation of the academies of Vienna and St Petersburg. He hoped in this way to get the support of royal and noble patrons for scientific and literary research.

Leibniz was in Paris from 1672 to 1676, except for a short visit which he paid to England in 1673. While in Paris he made a careful study of the Cartesian philosophy and of mathematics. He had much conversation with Malebranche on philosophy, and with Huyghens on physics and mechanics. He studied the mathematical works of Pascal, and invented a calculating machine to add, subtract, divide, and multiply.

During his visit to England in 1673 he was made a Fellow of the Royal Society, partly through the influence of his friend Robert Boyle, the chemist. Leibniz had read Hobbes's writings, and had been a good deal impressed by Hobbes's theories of physics. He wrote to Hobbes and hoped to see him during this visit. But Hobbes was eighty-five; he left the letter unanswered, and the two philosophers never met.

When he finally left Paris in October 1676 he went to London for a week and thence to Amsterdam, where he stayed for four weeks with Spinoza's friend and disciple Schuller. Leibniz had already in 1675 met Tschirnhausen, the most intelligent of Spinoza's correspondents, and had been interested by him in Spinoza's work. In November 1676 Spinoza, who was always very nervous of letting strangers see his unpublished writings, finally allowed Leibniz to meet him at The Hague. Leibniz stayed there for some time, had much talk with Spinoza, and pointed out to Spinoza certain fundamental mistakes in Descartes's mechanics. In return he was allowed to see some parts of the *Ethics* in manuscript. Later, when Leibniz had completed his own system, he became very critical of Spinozism. But at this time he had convinced himself that both Cartesianism and Hobbes's materialism were ultimately unsatisfactory, and he was ready to accept ideas from any quarter.

At the end of 1676 Leibniz was appointed librarian to the Duke of Brunswick at Hanover, a post which he held till the end of his life. The library at Hanover still contains masses of Leibniz's manuscripts on all kinds of subjects, which were slowly being published by the Berlin Academy until the Second World War. While there he carried on a voluminous correspondence with other learned men, e.g. Arnauld, John Bernoulli, de Volder, des Bosses, and Clarke. Leibniz's official duty was to write a history of the House of Brunswick. He travelled for some time in Italy collecting materials, for the first historical member of the Guelf family was Azo D'Este, and the noble Italian House of Este is a collateral line of the House of Brunswick.

Leibniz seems to have been working out his own system between 1680 and 1697, and to have been a good deal influenced during this period first by Plato and later by Aristotle. In 1698 his Duke of Brunswick died, and was succeeded by the man who became King of England in 1714 as George I. George was an ignorant boor, and he disliked Leibniz for busying himself with foreign monarchs in trying to found academies. And Leibniz lost two very good friends at the deaths of the two Electresses Sophia, George's mother and sister, who were highly intelligent and cultured women.

Leibniz completed his discovery of the differential calculus in 1676, but did not publish an account of it till 1684. Newton published his own form of the calculus in 1693. There was very acrimonious controversy about the discovery, though there is little doubt that in fact the two men made it independently of each other. Today in use is Leibniz's notation and not Newton's. Neither gave a logically flawless account of the principles of the calculus, but Newton was perhaps nearer the truth than Leibniz. The Newtonians in England poisoned George I's mind against Leibniz, and he failed to get the office of Historiographer Royal of England, which he had wanted. He died in 1716 in Hanover, almost in disgrace.

Leibniz was probably the most universal genius that there had ever been in Europe. He had none of the contempt for antiquity which characterized Descartes, Malebranche, Hobbes, Bacon, and Locke. He admired and learnt much from Plato and Aristotle, and he was thoroughly versed in the Scholastic philosophy. And, in general, he was extremely eclectic; though he had so much originality and such logical acumen that he thoroughly transformed and developed the germs which he got from others. He said that Descartes 'leads us into the vestibule of philosophy' and that Spinoza 'would be right if it were not for the monads'. He made an extremely careful study of Locke's *Essay*, and collected his criticisms into a large book – the *Nouveaux Essais*.[1] Locke treated his criticisms with a contempt which they certainly did not deserve. He also elaborately criticized Newton's theories of absolute space, time, and motion, in his *Correspondence with Clarke*, who acted as Newton's representative. Leibniz was a mathematician of the first rank. He made important contributions to the foundation of dynamics. He was one of the founders of modern symbolic logic. He tried to devise a geometrical calculus, and this afterwards became the starting-point of Grassmann's *Ausdehnungslehre*.[2] He sketched out the principle of a universal language of ideograms. He was also a very considerable jurist and historian. Among his minor achievements was to produce a geometrical argument to prove that the electors to the monarchy of Poland ought to choose Philip Augustus of Neuburg as king.

[1] [*Nouveaux Essais sur l'Entendement Humain*. G., V, 39–509. Langley, 41–629.]
[2] [H. Grassmann, *Die lineare Ausdehnungslehre, ein neuer Zweig der Mathematik* (Leipzig, 1844).]

2 Works

Leibniz wrote copiously, but very little was published in his lifetime and much is unpublished still. His most important philosophical works are probably the following:[1]

(1) *Discours de métaphysique* (written 1685, published 1846 by Grotefend).

(2) *Correspondence with Arnauld* (written 1686–90, published 1846 by Grotefend). The correspondence begins by Leibniz sending an abstract of the *Discours* to the Landgraf Ernst of Hessen-Rheinfels, and asking him to forward it to Arnauld.

(3) *The New System* (published in the *Journal des Savans* for 1695). This is the only complete account of his system which Leibniz ever published. It omits certain very fundamental considerations which are stressed in the *Discours* and the *Letters to Arnauld*. It led to a good deal of controversy, and Leibniz tried to explain and defend various points in it in later articles and letters.

(4) *Controversy with Pierre Bayle* (written in 1698 and round about 1703; published in 1716 in the *Histoire critique de la république des lettres* at the instance of des Maiseaux.) Bayle had criticized certain doctrines in *The New System* in the article on Rorarius in his *Dictionary* (1695–7); Leibniz answered; and Bayle raised further objections in the second edition of his *Dictionary* (1702). Leibniz answered these in turn.

(5) *Letters to John Bernoulli* (written about 1698; published first with many omissions in 1745). John Bernoulli was one of a family of extremely eminent mathematicians. The correspondence deals largely with infinity, continuity, and the nature of bodies.

(6) *Letters to de Volder* (written 1699–1706; first published by Gerhardt round about 1880). De Volder was Professor of Philosophy, Physics, and Mathematics at Leyden. He was a friend of John Bernoulli. He was an eminent Cartesian. The correspondence covers most of the main doctrines of Leibniz's philosophy.

(7) *Letters to des Bosses* (written 1706–16; published first by Dutens 1768). Des Bosses was a learned Jesuit teacher of theology at Hildesheim. Both he and Leibniz were interested in the doctrine of transubstantiation, which is held by Roman Catholics and rejected by Protestants. This gave rise to very elaborate and subtle discussion about the nature of substances in general and bodies in particular. In his correspondence Leibniz develops a theory about compound sub-

[1] [For further references see Bibliographical Note.]

stances, viz. the theory of the *Vinculum Substantiale*, which does not appear elsewhere in his works.

(8) *Theodicy* (published 1710). This is a huge book, published in Leibniz's lifetime, in which he elaborately tries to justify the ways of God to man.

(9) *Principles of Nature and of Grace* (written between 1712 and 1714 for Prince Eugen of Savoy; first published 1718) and *Monadology* (written about the same time, almost certainly for some other individual whose name is unknown; first published in 1720 in a German translation). These are short and clear but somewhat popular accounts of Leibniz's complete system in its final form, written as a help for readers who had been interested in the *Theodicy* and wanted to know more of Leibniz's philosophy as a whole.

(10) *Correspondence with Clarke* (written 1715–16; published first by Clarke in 1717). This deals mainly with the question whether space and time and motion are absolute or relative, and with other logical and philosophical topics connected with it.

3 Influence

It appears from the above list that many of Leibniz's most careful expositions of his system were not available to the public until long after his death. Nevertheless he had an immense influence in Germany. His philosophy was popularized and simplified by Wolff, and it became the orthodox system taught to students in German universities in the eighteenth century. Kant was brought up in it; he remained in it until Hume 'awoke him from his dogmatic slumbers'; and there are many traces of Leibnizian doctrines embedded in Kant's critical philosophy. The optimism of Leibniz's *Theodicy* is somewhat unfairly made fun of by Voltaire in the character of Dr Pangloss in *Candide*. Among later philosophers Herbart and Lotze in Germany and Ward and McTaggart in England were greatly influenced by Leibniz.

2

GENERAL PRINCIPLES USED BY LEIBNIZ

There are certain general principles of which Leibniz makes constant use. I shall begin by discussing these.

1 Predicate-in-Notion Principle

This plays a very important part in the *Discours de métaphysique* and the *Letters to Arnauld* (1685–90). It is not explicitly mentioned in *The New System* (1695) or in any of the later works that I have mentioned. But there is no reason to think that Leibniz himself ever abandoned it or ceased to think it of fundamental importance. From time to time he makes remarks which seem plainly to refer to it. E.g. in his *Second Answer to Bayle* (*c.* 1703) he says that in *The New System* he put forward the theory that each substance represents in itself all other substances in the world *simply as an explanatory hypothesis.*[1] But it is in fact *necessary,* for reasons which he had developed in his *Letters to Arnauld.* Again, in a letter of 19 August 1715 to des Bosses he says that it is of the essence of a substance that its present state should be pregnant with all its future states, and that from any one of its states all the others could be inferred unless God should interfere miraculously.[2]

The principle may be stated roughly as follows. Every substance has a complete notion, and the complete notion of it in some sense contains every fact about it down to the very minutest detail of its remotest future history. We will now consider it more in detail.

1.1 Complete notion of an individual

In his letter of 14 July 1686 to Arnauld, Leibniz tries to explain what he means by the complete notion of the actual Adam.[3] It is identical with 'the knowledge which God had of Adam when he determined to create him'.

---

[1] [G., IV, 554–71. Loemker, 574–85.]
[2] [G., II, 503. Loemker, 613.]
[3] [G., II, 47–59. Loemker, 331–8.]

Leibniz then points out that we must carefully distinguish between specific notions, e.g. that of the sphere or the ellipse, and individual notions, e.g. that of Adam. All true propositions about the subject of a specific notion are *necessary* and *independent of God's volitions*. But a specific notion is, in a certain sense, incomplete. It applies to an indefinite number of actual or possible individuals, and therefore does not provide an exclusive or an exhaustive description of any one of them. The notion of an individual is *complete*. It applies only to that individual, and it supplies an exhaustive as well as an exclusive description of it. It therefore always contains explicitly or implicitly predicates referring to determinate times and places and circumstances. True propositions which ascribe such predicates to an individual are *contingent* and they *depend on God's free decisions* at the time when he created the world. Therefore the complete notion of an actual individual must contain the fact that God made such-and-such free decisions.

Suppose now that we abstract from the notion of an actual individual the fact that it exists, and thus regard it as the notion of a merely possible individual. Then it is plain that the notion of this possible individual will contain the notions of these same free decisions of God, considered now as merely possible and not as actual.

It should be noted that Leibniz held that the actual laws of dynamics and the actual laws of human psychology express certain free decisions of God, subordinate to his primary decision to actualize the best on the whole of all the possible worlds. So I take it that the notion of the actual Adam would contain *inter alia* the actual laws of human psychology and of dynamics. If you want to conceive the actual Adam as a merely possible individual whom God might not have decided to actualize, you will still have to include in the notion of him the same laws, considered now as merely possible laws.

1.2 Alternative possible individuals

Leibniz often talks of alternative possible individuals with the same grammatical proper name, e.g. several alternative possible Adams. Arnauld says in his letter of 13 May 1686 that he finds such phrases very obscure.[1] If it be intelligible to talk of several alternative Adams, it should be equally intelligible to say that there were two alternative possible Arnaulds, one of whom would become a priest and remain single and childless (as the actual Arnauld did), and the other of whom would become a physician and marry and have several children. And

[1] [G., II, 25–34. Mason, 24–34.]

it should be intelligible to say that God deliberately actualized the first of these possible Arnaulds and deliberately left the second a mere unrealized possibility. Now such sentences seemed to Arnauld to be meaningless.

Arnauld's own view about merely possible substances may, I think, be put as follows. When one talks of a merely possible substance one is talking intelligibly only if one starts from the notion of one's actual substance, e.g. the actual Arnauld, and then proceeds as follows. (1) You may consider the nature of that substance in abstraction from its existence, and can imagine that that nature never had been endowed with existence. (2) You can imagine that certain of the potentialities involved in the nature of an actual substance had been actualized in certain ways instead of remaining permanently latent or conversely. E.g. you can imagine that the potentiality of the actual Arnauld to beget children had been exercised though in fact it was not; or that the same potentiality in his father had not been exercised though it in fact was. (3) You can imagine that certain of these potentialities, which were in fact exercised in certain ways, had been exercised instead in certain other ways. E.g. you can imagine that Arnauld's intellectual and practical gifts had been exercised in medicine instead of in theology.

Leibniz deals with these points in his letter of 14 July 1686.[1] He admits that the phrase 'several alternative possible Adams' is meaningless if you take the word 'Adam' to be the proper name of a certain completely determinate individual. But, when he uses the phrase, he takes the word 'Adam' to connote a certain limited collection of properties. These seem to us to describe uniquely a certain individual, but they do not in fact do so. E.g. we might take the word 'Adam' as denoting any individual who had the property of being a man without human parents, of having a woman created out of one of his ribs, and of disobeying God's orders by eating the fruit of a certain tree at the instigation of that woman. If the story in Genesis is true, that description does in fact apply to one and only one actual individual, and he has all the other properties possessed by the actual Adam. But we can obviously conceive without contradiction that these few properties (even if we include among them the actual laws of nature) might be supplemented in innumerable different alternative ways. Each such alternative supplementation would describe a possible individual, who might be called an 'alternative possible Adam'.

I think it is plain that this process could be generalized and applied

[1] [G., II, 47–59. Loemker, 331–8.]

to *any* actual substance. You start with any finite set of properties P_S, which together suffice to distinguish the actual substance S from all other actual substances. S will in fact have innumerable other properties beside these, and they will not all be entailed by the properties in P_S. You can therefore imagine this nucleus P_S to be supplemented in innumerable different alternative ways. You would thus conceive so many 'alternative possible S's'. Leibniz remarks that the only description which would suffice to distinguish the actual Adam, not only from all other *actual* individuals, but also from all other possible individuals, would be his complete notion, i.e. the sum-total of all his predicates.

Leibniz remarks that anything that is actual can be conceived as merely possible. If the actual Adam will in course of time have such-and-such a history and such-and-such descendants, the same properties will belong to the same Adam considered merely as one possibility among others. Anything is possible, Leibniz says, which is the subject of a genuine proposition; by which I take him to mean one that is not self-contradictory.

Now Leibniz frequently talks of alternative *possible worlds*. In the same letter he tries to explain what he means by this. Each possible world corresponds to certain possible *primary* ends or intentions characteristic of it. If God had decided to actualize a certain possible world, he would have made certain *primary* free decisions, embodying the main ends or intentions characteristic of that world. These would have been the most general principles constituting the ground-plan of that world. The notions of all the individual substances in that world would be determined in view of these primary intentions. If there were to be miracles in the course of that world's history, they too could have been determined from the beginning in accordance with these primary intentions. For a miracle would be an exception only to certain *secondary* principles which God willed in view of his primary intentions in creating that world.

1.3 Various formulations of the Principle

Leibniz formulates the Predicate-in-Notion Principle in various places. The main statement in the *Discours de métaphysique* is in Section 8.[1] The essential points which he makes there are the following. The predicate of every true affirmative proposition is contained, either explicitly or implicitly, in its subject. If it is contained explicitly, the

[1] [G., IV, 432-3. Loemker, 307-8.]

proposition is analytical. If it is contained only implicitly, the proposition is synthetic. It is a characteristic property of an individual substance to have a notion so complete that anyone who fully understood it could infer from it all the predicates, down to the minutest detail and the remotest future, which will ever belong to that substance. Leibniz takes the case of Alexander the Great as an example. In contemplating the complete notion of Alexander, God sees in it the foundation or reason for every predicate which can ever be truly ascribed to him. In this way God knows *a priori* whether, e.g., Alexander will die by wounds or by disease or of old age. But no *man* can fully and distinctly comprehend the notion of any individual substance. So men have to depend on experience or on hearsay for their knowledge of many of the facts about individuals. Thus, e.g., men who died before Alexander's death never knew for certain how he would die; his contemporaries had to wait and see; and his successors knew only by traditions which go back to contemporary eye-witnesses.

In his letter to Arnauld of 14 July 1686, Leibniz says that we need a 'reason *a priori*' to enable us to say that the same individual who was in Paris last week is in Germany this week.[1] He alleges that the only possible *a priori* reason for such statements is that the notion of that individual contains and connects these two successive and separated events. In the same letter he says: 'In every true proposition, necessary or contingent, universal or singular, the notion of the predicate is contained in some way in the subject. If not, I do not know what truth is.'[2] It would appear from this that Leibniz thinks that the Principle emerges from, and is justified by, reflecting on what is meant by a proposition being true.

2 Principle of Sufficient Reason

What Leibniz calls the *Principle of Sufficient Reason* is so closely bound up with the Predicate-in-Notion Principle that it seems desirable to consider it before making any criticisms on the former.

In Section 13 of the *Discours de métaphysique*, Leibniz says that for every *contingent* fact there is a reason why the fact is so and not otherwise.[3] He adds that this is equivalent to the principle that for every contingent fact there is a proof *a priori* which would show that the

[1] [G., II, 53. Loemker, 335.]
[2] [G., II, 56. Loemker, 337.]
[3] [G., IV, 436–9. Loemker, 310–11.]

connexion of the subject and the predicate in the fact is founded on the natures of these two terms.

In his letter of 14 July 1686 to Arnauld, shortly after the passage that I have quoted above in connexion with the Predicate-in-Notion Principle, Leibniz writes as follows:[1] 'There must always be some foundation for the connexion of the terms of a proposition which is true, and this foundation must be in the notions of the terms.' He describes this as 'my great principle'. He thinks that all philosophers would accept it, but that most of them have failed to draw its many important consequences. He says that one of these is the generally accepted principle: 'Nothing happens without it being possible to give a reason why it happened as it did and not in another way.'[2] He adds that such reasons 'often incline without necessitating'.[3] The latter is a rather mysterious phrase which he often uses. We may now consider Leibniz's various statements in turn:

(1) Of Leibniz's various statements the least determinate seems to be what he calls 'my great principle', viz. that there must always be *some* foundation for the connexion between the terms of any true proposition, and that this foundation must be in the notions of the terms. We might call this the *Principle of Grounded Connexion*.

(2) It seems that Leibniz then makes this more definite by specifying the nature of the foundation. The specific principle is that in every true affirmative proposition, necessary or contingent, universal or singular, the notion of the predicate is contained either explicitly or implicitly in the subject. This is the *Predicate-in-Notion Principle*. As we saw, Leibniz says that it seems to him evident when he considers what is meant by a proposition being true.

(3) Every substance has a notion so complete that anyone who fully understood it could infer from it all the predicates, down to the minutest detail, which will ever belong to that substance. I think that Leibniz would regard this as an immediate consequence of applying the Predicate-in-Notion Principle to the special case of true affirmative propositions about *individual substances*. We might call this the *Principle of Pre-determinate Individual History*.

(4) For every contingent fact there is a reason why the fact is so and not otherwise, but such reasons often incline without necessitating. This is the *Principle of Sufficient Reason*. Leibniz says that this is equivalent to the principle that for every contingent fact there is a proof *a priori* which would show that the connexion between the subject and the predicate is founded on the natures of those terms. Thus the

[1] [G., II, 56. Loemker, 337.]   [2] [ibid.]   [3] [ibid.]

Principle of Sufficient Reason seems to be an immediate application of the Principle of Grounded Connexion to the particular case of *contingent* propositions or facts. I do not doubt that Leibniz would have held that there is also a sufficient reason for every *necessary* fact, and that here also there is a proof *a priori* which would show that the connexion between subject and predicate is founded on the natures of those terms. But he would not think it necessary to include in his Principle of Sufficient Reason this further statement, which no one would be likely to question. What he wanted to emphasize was his view, which many people would find highly paradoxical, that there is a proof *a priori* even in the case of contingent facts. And he wishes to make explicit a certain important peculiarity here, which he expresses by the mysterious phrase about 'reasons inclining without necessitating'.

3 Is the Predicate-in-Notion Principle compatible with contingency?

There is no doubt that Leibniz held that there are genuinely contingent facts or true propositions. And there is no doubt that he held that the Predicate-in-Notion Principle applies to *all* facts and true propositons. He realizes that it might seem as if the Principle was incompatible with there being any contingent facts. He tries to deal with this point in Section 13 of the *Discours de métaphysique*.[1] His argument is as follows.

We must distinguish between *absolutely* and *hypothetically* necessary connexions. When the connexion between the subject and the predicate of a proposition is absolutely necessary the contradictory of the proposition is *self*-contradictory. When the connexion is only hypothetically necessary the contradictory of the proposition is *not* self-contradictory, and the proposition is contingent. A hypothetically necessary connexion between two terms is founded, not simply on the natures of the two, but also on certain voluntary decisions which God has freely made. Of these free decisions the most fundamental one is that God has decided to actualize that possible world which is on the whole more perfect than any other alternative possible world. Certain other decisions of a more special character are subordinate to this, in the sense that God would have been *practically inconsistent* if he had willed this and had not willed these. They are, nevertheless, free. Thus, e.g., a man who has freely decided to take a certain examination is still free not to read any of the set books or to attend any of the prescribed lectures. But, unless he makes and keeps to the subordinate

[1] [G., IV, 436–9. Loemker, 310–11.]

decisions to read the books and attend the lectures, he is behaving in a practically inconsistent way. A man can be, and often is, practically inconsistent; but this is a defect in him. God *could be* practically inconsistent, but we can be sure that he always acts and wills consistently.

According to Leibniz, the laws of human psychology and the laws of dynamics represent secondary decisions which God has freely made in view of his primary decision to actualize the best of all the possible worlds. Now every connexion which is founded to any extent on such decrees is only hypothetically necessary. The corresponding true proposition is contingent, although it could in theory be known with complete certainty. It could be known with certainty because we can be quite sure that God has chosen to actualize the best possible world, and that he has made and acted upon all such subordinate decisions as are required in view of this primary one. It is none the less contingent, because these decisions are made *freely* by God. God rejected the alternatives which he did reject, not because they involved internal contradiction and were *intrinsically* impossible, but because they were *less perfect* on the whole than a certain other possible alternative, and he had freely decided to actualize the best of the possible worlds.

He sums up his discussion of this point at the end of Section 13 of the *Discours* as follows. All such difficulties are met if one bears in mind two things. (1) For every contingent fact there is a proof *a priori* which would show that the connexion of the subject and the predicate in the fact is founded on their natures. (2) On the other hand, these proofs *a priori* of contingent propositions are not demonstrations that they are necessary. For the reasons in all such cases involve an appeal to what Leibniz calls 'the principle of contingency or of the existence of things'. This is the primary principle that God chooses that which is *actually* best of the alternatives which are *really* possible; and the subordinate principle that every man chooses that which *seems to him at the time* to be the best of the alternatives which then *seem* to him to be possible. In the case of necessary facts the proof is based on the law of contradiction and on the absolute necessity of the terms being related as subject and predicate, without reference to the free volitions of God or of his creatures.

In his letter of 13 May 1686 Arnauld asked Leibniz to say definitely which of the following alternatives he accepts.[1] (1) Is the connexion between Adam and his predicates intrinsic and necessary, like the

¹ [G., II, 28–30. Mason, 27–9.]

connexion between the defining properties of a circle and any other property which is common and peculiar to all possible circles? Or (2) is it dependent on the free decrees of God? Leibniz, in his answer of 14 July 1686, says that he cannot admit that the two alternatives are mutually exclusive and collectively exhaustive.[1] The connexion between Adam, on the one hand, and all that will ever happen to him, on the other, *is* intrinsic, but it is *not* necessary independently of the free decrees of God. His argument is as follows.

The notion of a possible Adam involves *inter alia* the notion of certain possible free decrees of God. Leibniz agrees with Arnauld that anything that is possible at all is so independently of the *actual* volitions of God. But the notion of a *possible* existent involves the notion of certain *possible* volitions of God. For the possibility of a contingent fact or of an individual existent presupposes the possibility of its cause; and, in the long run, these possible causes are the possible volitions of God. On the other hand, the possibility of a necessary fact or of a species (e.g. the circle) involves no reference even to God's possible volitions.

Arnauld also raised an objection which may be put as follows. Suppose that the predicate of taking a certain journey to Paris at a certain moment *t* were contained in the notion of the actual Arnauld. And suppose that the word 'Arnauld' was used to denote the same individual in the two sentences 'Arnauld started for Paris at *t*' and 'Arnauld did not start for Paris at *t*.' Then the latter sentence would express a proposition which is not merely false but *self-contradictory*, and the former would express a proposition which is not merely true but tautologous. But this is plainly false. Therefore the predicate of starting for Paris at *t*, though it does in fact belong to the actual Arnauld, is not contained in the complete notion of him. This is not altered by the fact, which Arnauld admits, that God knew from the first that Arnauld would start for Paris at *t*. (In order to avoid confusion here the following point should be noticed. On the assumption that the word 'Arnauld' denotes the same individual in both sentences, the propositions expressed by them certainly *contradict each other*. But this is irrelevant. The point is that neither of them expresses a proposition which is *self*-contradictory or *tautologous*.)

Leibniz's answer is as follows. He agrees that there is no general property possessed by Arnauld (comparable to the definition of a circle) from which it *necessarily follows* that he will start for Paris at *t*. But, since it has *always* been certain that he will do so (for otherwise

[1] [G., II, 50-1. Loemker, 333.]

God could not have known it beforehand) there must be *some* timeless connexion between Arnauld (the subject) and starting for Paris at *t* (the predicate). If he were not to take that journey at that time, this would destroy the notion which God had of him when he decided to create him. For that notion, considered as the notion of an as yet merely possible individual, includes all the future facts about Arnauld and all the decrees of God on which these facts would depend, considered also as merely possible. On the other hand, says Leibniz, the supposition that Arnauld did not start for Paris at *t* would not conflict with any *necessary* truth.

Arnauld reinforced the argument which we have been discussing with an epistemological argument, which may be stated as follows. Each person has in his own mind a clear and distinct idea of himself. Now, if you have a clear and distinct idea of anything, you can discover with complete certainty, by inspecting your idea, what the notion of that thing does and does not contain. Now, when Arnauld inspects his idea of himself, he sees clearly that e.g. the power of thinking *is* contained in it. But he sees equally clearly that the property of taking a certain journey at a certain date is *not*. Nothing would have been Arnauld that did not have the power of thinking; but Arnauld can see by inspection that an individual could have been Arnauld without starting for Paris at *t*. The fact that God foresaw from the first that Arnauld would start for Paris at *t* is irrelevant to the question whether doing so is contained in the complete notion of Arnauld.

Leibniz's answer is as follows. It is not at all surprising that mere inspection of the idea which one has of oneself will not enable one to know with certainty whether one will or will not make a certain journey at a certain date. The complete notion of any individual is infinitely complex. Therefore the idea which any human being can have of any individual (whether it be himself or another) is inevitably confused. But the notion of a species, e.g. the sphere, contains a finite nucleus of defining properties from which all the other properties follow of necessity. It is therefore possible for a human being to have a distinct idea of the sphere. And so it is possible to decide with certainty whether a given geometrical property does or does not belong to spheres as such. No such certainty is possible in regard to the future action of an individual. 'Otherwise,' says Leibniz, 'it would be as easy to be a prophet as to be a geometer.'

4 Comments on the Predicate-in-Notion Principle

I shall now make some comments on the Predicate-in-Notion Principle and on some of the ideas which are associated with it.

4.1 Complete notion of a species

It will be best to start with what Leibniz would call a 'specific' notion, as distinct from the notion of an individual. We shall need to take several examples, and we will begin with the notion of a certain kind of geometrical figure, viz. the circle.

4.1.1 Geometrical figures

There is an unlimited number of geometrical properties which belong to all circles and only to circles. I think that Leibniz would say that the complete notion of the circle consists of all these properties and only of these. Now one and only one of these would commonly be said to be what the word 'circle' means; viz. the property of being a plane curve all of whose points are equidistant from a certain fixed point. I think that Leibniz would call this property 'the essence of the circle', and he would say that it constitutes 'the *real* definition', as opposed to various possible '*nominal* definitions' of the circle. A nominal definition would be any property which belongs to all circles and only to circles, but is not the meaning of the word 'circle'.

Now I think that Leibniz would say that, in the case of the circle, all the other properties in the complete notion follow necessarily from the property which is the real definition. Consider now any sentence of the form 'The circle has the property P', which expresses a true proposition. Here 'P' must stand either for the defining property or for one of the other properties in the complete notion. If it stood for the defining property or for any part of it, I think that Leibniz would say that it is *explicitly* contained in the notion of the circle. If it stood for any other property common and peculiar to circles, I think he would say that it is *implicitly* contained in the notion of the circle. But in either case, he would say, the proposition is necessary and independent of God's free decrees, whether actual or possible.

Before taking other examples I will make the following remarks on this one. (1) Suppose that we had taken as an example the ellipse instead of the circle. None of the innumerable geometrical properties which are common and peculiar to ellipses as such can plausibly be singled out as the *meaning* of the word 'ellipse'. Thus the ellipse has a complete notion; and, if you choose any one property from it, all the rest follow in the same sense in which all the other properties of the circle follow from its defining property. But none of them can be singled out as the 'essence' or 'real definition' of the ellipse. (2) In the case of the circle the defining property follows from any other property in its complete notion in precisely the same sense in which any other property in its complete notion follows from its defining property.

These considerations lead one to suspect that it is a very contingent fact that there is a certain outstanding property in the case of the circle which can plausibly be taken as its agreed or real definition. It seems to depend on the fact that there happens to be one and only one property in the complete notion which almost hits one in the eye in this case. So the distinction between predicates which are contained explicitly and those which are contained only implicitly in the notion of a certain species of geometrical figures turns out to be largely arbitrary. It depends on which of them you take as the defining property, and generally there seems to be no objective ground for taking one rather than another.

(3) Even in the case of the circle it is not strictly true to say that the other properties follow necessarily from the defining property. The presence of the other properties follows from the presence of the defining property *together with* the axioms of Euclidean geometry. I think therefore that Leibniz would have to say that the complete notion of the circle, or of any other kind of geometrical figure, contains *inter alia* the axioms of Euclidean geometry. Leibniz would no doubt have regarded these axioms as necessary propositions, true in all possible worlds, and therefore independent of God's free decrees and not needing to be specifically mentioned any more than the laws of logic.

But we know better now. We know that other sets of axioms, inconsistent in certain respects with Euclid's, are self-consistent. If you take the same definition of a circle, and combine it in one case with the axioms of Euclid and in another with those of Lobachevski, some of the properties entailed will be the same but others will be different. E.g. the circumference of a Euclidean circle is proportional to its radius, whilst that of a Lobachevskian circle is not.

You will remember that Leibniz says that the notion of each alternative possible Adam would contain certain possible free decrees of God characteristic of the possible world of which it is a member. It is now clear that we must also talk of alternative possible kinds of circle. We must say that the notion of each alternative possible kind of circle contains certain possible free decrees of God which would fix the geometry of a certain possible world. The same remarks would apply *mutatis mutandis* to any other kind of geometrical figure.

4.1.2 Arithmetical notions

If we want an example of a specific notion in which all the predicates are *necessarily* connected, and the necessity is *absolute* and not hypothetical, we must leave geometry and go to pure arithmetic. Take, e.g., the notion of prime numbers. The accepted definition of this is an integer which is not exactly divisible by any other integer except unity. The complete notion of a prime number would consist of all those properties and only those which belong to entities answering to this definition. An example of such a property is that the immediate successor of the product of all the integers below it is divisible by it. (Wilson's Theorem). This property is not contained explicitly in the notion of a prime number, i.e. it is not a part of its defining property. But it is contained implicitly, in so far as it follows from the defining property, together with principles which are all propositions of logic or pure arithmetic and therefore necessary and independent of God's volitions.

I think that we can now understand Leibniz's distinction between 'absolutely' and 'conditionally' necessary propositions. Suppose that P is the defining property of a subject S. Suppose that Q is another property. It might be that 'S is Q' follows from 'S is P' *alone*, as, e.g., *Negroes are men* follows from *Negroes are black men*. Failing this, it might be that 'S is Q' follows from a combination of 'S is P' with one or more propositions, all of which are *necessary*. In both these cases Leibniz would say that 'S is Q' is *absolutely* necessary. In the former he would say that Q is *explicitly* contained in S; in the latter that it is *implicitly* contained in S. Lastly, suppose that 'S is Q' follows from the combination of 'S is P' with one or more propositions which are all true in the actual world but are not all necessary. Then Leibniz would call such propositions *hypothetically* necessary.

4.1.3 Natural kinds

We will next consider the sort of species which Mill calls 'natural kinds'. It might be a certain kind of matter, e.g. gold. Or it might be a vegetable or animal species, e.g. oak-tree or horse.

It is a fact about the actual world that there are certain small groups of properties about which the following propositions are true: (1) Any two things which have all the properties in such a group have innumerable other properties in common, and differ only in comparatively minor and unimportant respects. (2) If one thing has all the properties in such a group and another thing lacks any of them, then the two will differ in a great many major respects. Take, e.g., the two properties of melting at 1062°C and having a density of 19·26 gm per/cc. Any two bits of matter which have these two properties agree also in having all the innumerable chemical and physical properties characteristic of gold. Any such small group of properties constitutes what we will call a *'sufficient description'* of a natural kind.

The complete notion of a natural kind will consist of a sufficient description of it, together with all the other properties common and peculiar to all substances which answer to that sufficient description. If the omission or the appreciable modification of any property in a sufficient description of a natural kind would make it insufficient, we will call it a *'minimal* sufficient description'. Lastly, we must notice that the same natural kind may have many different minimal sufficient descriptions. E.g. the two properties 'rational animal' and 'featherless biped' are alternative minimal sufficient descriptions of the species *man.*

It is only because of these contingent facts about the clustering together of properties in the actual world that it is practicable and useful to have specific names like 'man', 'gold', etc. And it is only because of such facts that we can talk of 'definitions' of such names. It is usual, e.g., to give 'rational animal' as the definition of *man.* Really it is only one minimal sufficient description. It satisfies us because in the actual world these properties carry with them the characteristic human form and all the other properties which are associated in our minds with the word 'man'.

Speaking in Leibnizian terms we may say that the notion of a natural kind contains *inter alia* the notion of a free decree of God to associate together a certain cluster of characteristics in the way which I have described. In one of the possible worlds, e.g., the property of being a rational animal would be associated, not with the other properties which are characteristic of men, but with those that are characteristic of parrots. In that world there would be nothing that we should call men, but there would be a species which we should call 'rational parrots'.

There is *prima facie* at least one important difference between a species of geometrical figures and a natural kind. All the other properties of the circle, e.g., follow from any minimum sufficient description of it together with the axioms of geometry in the world under consideration. And these axioms are not specially concerned with *circles*; they are extremely general propositions about spatial order and interconnexion. But we do not know, e.g., of any general proposition about the actual world which, in combination with the proposition *x has two legs and no feathers*, entails the proposition *x is rational*. Thus, to speak in Leibnizian terms, the notion of any one natural kind seems to involve a number of very special divine decrees directly associating certain properties with certain others. But the notion of any one kind of geometrical figure seems to involve no special divine decrees peculiar to it. It involves only very general divine decrees about the spatial order and interconnexion of a certain possible world.

4.2 Complete notion of an individual

We can now leave specific notions and consider the notion of an *individual*, e.g. Adam or Arnauld. A very important new feature which enters at this point is that we now have to take account of *singular* propositions, which involve perfectly determinate dates and may involve perfectly determinate places; e.g. *Queen Elizabeth sneezed at 5 p.m. on Christmas Day 1597*.

The next point to notice is that the notion of an individual is the notion of something which persists for a finite time, however short; and which is in a perfectly determinate state in respect of each of its determinable characteristics at every moment of its history. Its states at every moment between two assigned moments may be all exactly alike, or they may not. In the former case we should say that the individual has remained unchanged between the two moments; in the latter that it has changed, either suddenly or continuously, between them. But in either case the notion of any individual involves an infinite number of singular propositions specifying its states at a continuous series of moments. It is therefore plain, as Leibniz asserts, that no human being could have an adequate and distinct idea of the complete notion of any individual, whether actual or possible.

The various propositions which are true of an individual, e.g. a certain bit of gold, are of two different kinds, viz. *non-dispositional* and *dispositional*. It is a non-dispositional proposition that it has a certain temperature at a certain moment. It is a dispositional proposition that, *if and only if* at any time its temperature should be at or above 1062°C, it *would* then be liquid. The dispositional propositions which are true of an individual are of various orders of generality. Some hold equally of *all* bits of matter, e.g. the law of inertia. Some are true only of the particular kind of matter, e.g. gold, to which the individual belongs, e.g. that it would melt at 1062°C. We must also contemplate the possibility of dispositional propositions which are *peculiar* to an individual, and are not deducible from more general ones together with the non-dispositional propositions which are true of it. There might, e.g., be certain dispositional propositions which are true of a certain person and are not deducible from the general laws of human psychology together with non-dispositional facts about that person.

It is plain that not all the propositions which are true of an individual are logically independent of each other. The proposition: *This bit of gold is liquid at the instant t* follows logically from *This bit of gold has a temperature of 1062°C at t* and *The melting point of gold is 1062°C*. We can therefore conceive a sub-class of propositions chosen on the following principles out of the sum-total of propositions which are true of a certain individual. (1) No proposition in the set is to be entailed by any combination of the others in the set. (2) Every true proposition about the individual which is *not* contained in the set is to be entailed by some combination of the propositions which *are* contained in it. I will call any such set a 'nuclear sub-set' for that individual. There might, of course, be many alternative nuclear sub-sets for the same individual.

Any nuclear sub-set would suffice to distinguish an individual, not only from every other actual individual, but also from every other *possible* individual. That is because a nuclear sub-set entails *all* the other propositions which are true of the individual. A selection of propositions which is non-nuclear may suffice to distinguish an actual individual from all other *actual* individuals, or to distinguish a possible individual from all other possible individuals which belong to the *same possible world*. Thus, e.g., the property of being a man without human parents suffices to distinguish the actual Adam from all other actual individuals. But it does not entail all the other predicates which belong to the actual Adam, and it does not suffice to distinguish the actual Adam from all other *possible* individuals. Speaking in Leibnizian terms, we might say that every proposition in a nuclear sub-set is the expression of a free decree of God, actual or possible, in regard to the actual or possible world of which the individual in question is a member.

Before summarizing this account of what is meant by the *complete notion of an individual* I will define the sense in which I shall use the word 'predicate'. Suppose that a certain bit of gold was sometimes solid and sometimes liquid. I shall call 'solidity' and 'liquidity' *characteristics*, and not predicates, of the gold. I shall say that being liquid on each different occasion was a different *predicate* of the gold. We might call the kind of predicate which is expressed by the phrase 'having the characteristic Q at the moment *t*' an '*instantaneous predicate*'. Besides these there are various kinds of *temporally generalized predicates*, e.g. 'characterized by Q sometimes', 'characterized by Q always', 'characterized by Q at all moments between t_1 and t_2'; and so on. It should be noted that a dispositional characteristic may be either permanent or variable. Thus a bit of pure iron has the same melting point at all times and under all circumstances; but under certain conditions it is magnetic for a period, and under other circumstances it is non-magnetic for a period. On the other hand, the characteristic of being magnetizable and demagnetizable under certain conditions belongs to a bit of iron at every moment.

I will now summarize the position as follows. The complete notion of an individual consists of every predicate of it which refers to any moment in its history. This collection will always contain predicates of two different kinds, viz. non-dispositional and dispositional. The dispositional characteristics will be of various orders of generality, and it is possible that some of them may be peculiar to the individual in question. Within the complete notion of an individual there will be one or more nuclear sub-sets. Any nuclear sub-set consists of predicates which are (1) logically independent of each other, and (2) together entail all the other predicates in the complete notion. A nuclear sub-set will always contain both dispositional and non-dispositional predicates. The predicates in a nuclear sub-set would suffice to distinguish an individual from all other individuals, actual or possible. But an actual individual may be distinguished from all other *actual* individuals, though not from all other *possible* individuals, by a selection of predicates which do not constitute a nuclear sub-set.

4.2.1 Does every individual have a complete notion?

This question reduces to the following. Does the phrase 'every predicate of an individual which refers to any moment of its history' denote a genuine collection which is, in some intelligible sense, complete at every moment, including those moments (if such there be) before this individual began to exist? Evidently Leibniz thought that the answer is *Yes*.

The case for an affirmative answer can be put most plausibly as follows. Suppose it is a fact that Queen Elizabeth sneezed at 5 p.m. on Christmas Day 1597. Then anyone who at any moment before then had said 'Queen Elizabeth *will* sneeze at 5 p.m. on Christmas Day 1597' would have been speaking truly. And anyone who at any moment after then had said: 'Queen Elizabeth *did* sneeze at 5 p.m. on Christmas Day 1597' would have been speaking truly. If we consider these sentences, and the beliefs which they would correctly express, we find that we can distinguish a *common content* and a *difference of tense*. We can also distinguish between what might be called the *time of occurrence* and the *time of reference*. The common content refers to an individual (Queen Elizabeth), a characteristic (sneezing), and a date. That date is the date of reference. The difference of tense is expressed by the difference between the copulas 'will', 'is now', and 'did'. It seems plausible to suggest that the common content is a fact about Queen Elizabeth and sneezing and the date of reference, which, although it *contains* that date as a constituent, *has* itself no date of occurrence. Such a fact might be expressed by the formula 'S is tenselessly characterized by Q at t.' The various beliefs or utterances, with their various dates of occurrence, are made true by corresponding with this tenseless fact about an individual, a characteristic, and a date of reference. The differences in tense correspond to the temporal relation between the date of occurrence of the belief or utterance and the date of reference which is a constituent in the fact of tenseless characterization, Thus, e.g., the total fact which corresponds to a true belief at t_1 that S will be characterized by Q at t_2 consists of two facts; viz. (1) the fact that S is tenselessly characterized by Q at t_2, and (2) the fact that t_1 is tenselessly earlier than t_2. There are two and only two kinds of change which can happen to a fact of tenseless characterization. One is that the date of reference in it alters continually in respect of the purely temporal property of pastness, presentness, and futurity. It becomes less and less remotely future, then present, and then more and more remotely past. But the fact itself, having no date of occurrence, undergoes no such change. The other change is that, whilst such a fact cannot be *known* by any human being at any date earlier than the date of reference in it, it may become known from time to time at any date which is *not* earlier than that date.

This line of argument, for what it is worth, is quite independent of theological considerations. But Leibniz would no doubt have added that God knew at every moment before 5 p.m. on Christmas Day 1597 that Queen Elizabeth would then sneeze. Therefore, he would say, there must have been this fact or true proposition to be the object of God's acts of knowing at each of these moments.

4.2.2 The ontological correlate of the complete notion

Leibniz thinks that many important and surprising ontological consequences follow from the principle that every individual has a complete notion which contains all its predicates. It is not easy to believe that any important ontological consequences could be entailed by such an extremely general logical principle alone. One is inclined to think that other principles must have been unwittingly combined with it in Leibniz's mind.

I suspect the reasoning at the back of Leibniz's mind may be illustrated as follows. Since it was already true when Queen Elizabeth was first created that she would sneeze at 5 p.m. on Christmas Day 1597, she must have been created with a certain special modification corresponding to this fact about her. Since it is true at every moment of her history up to the date of reference that she will sneeze at that date, this modification must have persisted up to then. And, since it is true at every moment after that date that she did sneeze then, the same modification must persist in her as long as she continues to exist. The persistent modification in the *actual substance* is, so to speak, the *ontological correlate* of the fact of tenseless characterization in the *complete notion* of the substance. Now all that happens to the fact of tenseless characterization is that the date, which is its temporal constituent, becomes less and less remotely future, then present, and then more and more remotely past. Similarly, all that happens to the correlated modification of the substance is its emergence from quiescence into activity and its subsequent reversion to quiescence. Corresponding to every non-dispositional fact of tenseless characterization in the notion of a substance there would be a special modification of the substance. This persists throughout the whole of its history, explodes into activity at the moment when the date of reference in the fact becomes present, and then reverts for ever into quiescence.

Now this kind of theory or picture is quite familiar in regard to dispositional properties. The conditional fact 'If a bit of gold were at any time raised to 1062°C, it would then melt' is commonly believed to correspond to a certain persistent structural peculiarity present in every bit of gold at every moment of its history. This kind of persistent modification may, however, burst into activity on many occasions. It will do so whenever the conditions mentioned in the antecedent of the conditional fact are fulfilled. Cf. also the theory of persistent traces in connexion with memory.

It seems to me plain that Leibniz thinks of any substance as coming into existence with a stock of innate modifications corresponding (1) to every non-dispositional fact of tenseless characterization referring to any moment in its history, and (2) to every dispositional fact about it, whether referring to every moment or to certain periods in its history. This seems to me to be the suppressed premiss which has to be combined with the Predicate-in-Notion Principle if one is to draw from it anything like the ontological consequences which Leibniz drew.

It seems plain to me that it is an independent premiss. It may have been suggested to Leibniz by the Predicate-in-Notion Principle, and he may have seen no other way in which the complete notion of a possible substance could be embodied in that substance when it was actualized by God's creative act. But I do not think that one can pretend that it is logically entailed by the Predicate-in-Notion Principle.

4.3 Is the Predicate-in-Notion Principle compatible with there being contingent facts?

In discussing this question it will be best to begin by considering certain sentences. We may call the sentence 'The Protestant daughter of Henry VIII was a Protestant' *explicitly analytic*. The sentences 'Queen Elizabeth was a Protestant' and 'The unmarried daughter of Henry VIII was a Protestant' are not explicitly analytic. But that is also true of the sentence 'The sun rises in the east.' If we consider this last sentence, we can raise the following question. What do we understand by 'east'? Does it mean just 'the quarter in which the sun rises'? If we substitute this *definiens* for the word 'east', the sentence becomes explicitly analytic. But suppose that we take the word 'east' to be defined by reference to the way in which a suspended compass-needle sets itself. Then substitution of the *definiens* does not make the sentence explicitly analytic.

Suppose now that a sentence, which is not explicitly analytic, contains a word or phrase which has a commonly accepted definition or description. Suppose that, when this definition or description is substituted for that word or phrase, the sentence becomes explicitly analytic. Then I should call the original sentence *implicitly analytic*. Thus, if the commonly accepted definition or description of 'east' is 'the quarter in which the sun rises', the sentence 'The sun rises in the east' is implicitly analytic. A sentence might have to be transformed in several successive stages before it becomes explicitly analytic. If a sentence is neither explicitly nor implicitly analytic, we will call it *synthetic*.

Now a sentence like 'Queen Elizabeth was a Protestant' or 'The unmarried daughter of Henry VIII was a Protestant' is certainly not explicitly analytic. Again, since a grammatical proper name, like 'Queen Elizabeth', has no commonly accepted definition or description, the former sentence is not implicitly analytic. Lastly, no substitution of commonly accepted definitions or descriptions for the word 'Protestant' or the phrase 'unmarried daughter' will make the second sentence explicitly analytic. So these two sentences are synthetic. The same is true of any sentence whose grammatical subject is the grammatical proper name of an individual. And it is true of most sentences in which the grammatical subject is a phrase which uniquely describes an individual.

When a person refers to an historical individual by a grammatical proper name, such as 'Queen Elizabeth', he must have at the back of his mind some sort of description of the individual in question. It might of course merely be of the form 'the person who is referred to in books on English history as "Queen Elizabeth" '. For it is plain that no grammatical proper name, used of an individual whom one has never met, can possibly function as a *logical* proper name, as the word 'that' might do if one pointed to a certain visible object and said 'That is a cow.' So, for the present purpose, the sentence 'Queen Elizabeth was a Protestant' is really equivalent to a sentence of the form 'The person who answered to such and such a description was a Protestant.'

Now in general one does not know what description is at the back of a person's mind when he utters or understands such a sentence. Often the person himself would be hard put to it to say what it is. Perhaps the most that can be said is that a certain complex mental disposition, which he has acquired in the course of his reading, is active at the time. This checks him and gives him a feeling of intellectual discomfort if he uses the name himself or hears it used by others outside a certain limited range of contexts. The description which is attached to the name will almost certainly vary from person to person and from one occasion to another with the same person. It might happen for a certain person on a certain occasion to include the property of being a Protestant. He might, e.g., be thinking of Queen Elizabeth as the first Protestant queen of England in her own right. If so, we might say that the sentence would be, for that person and on that occasion, implicitly analytic, in spite of the fact that the name 'Queen Elizabeth' has no commonly accepted definition or description.

In general, if a proposition about a term is to be necessary, the following conditions must be fulfilled. (1) The term must have a commonly accepted definition or description. (2) The proposition in question must be entailed either by this definition or description alone, or by it in combination with premisses all of which are necessary. It is plain that these conditions are not fulfilled in the case of most singular propositions about individuals. No individual has a definition, and in the case of most of them there is nothing that could be called a generally accepted description. And, even if the first condition were fulfilled, the second would break down as regards most singular propositions about individuals.

Now the Predicate-in-Notion Principle, as I have interpreted it, asserts that there is for every individual a collection of facts of the form 'S is tenselessly characterized by Q at t'; and that each such fact, though it contains a date of reference as a constituent, has no date of occurrence but subsists timelessly. I think it is plain that this does not entail that an individual has a generally accepted definition or description. And it does not entail that, if an individual had such a definition or description, every true proposition about it would follow either from this alone or from this in conjunction with premisses all of which are necessary. The Principle is therefore compatible with there being contingent facts.

4.4 Is the Predicate-in-Notion Principle compatible with human freedom?

The Principle might be compatible with there being contingent facts and yet incompatible with human freedom. Freedom is impossible without contingency, but contingency does not entail freedom. The fact that Vesuvius erupted and destroyed Pompei in A.D. 79 would be held by Leibniz and by many other philosophers to be contingent, but no one regards it as a free act on the part of the volcano.

If the Predicate-in-Notion Principle is true, the future is already *determinate*. It was true at the time of Romulus and Remus that Julius Caesar would decide at a certain future date to cross the Rubicon. But this leaves entirely open the question whether Caesar's decision was *causally determined*. That is a question about the connexion of that event with contemporary and earlier events and relationships and with

Julius Caesar's dispositional properties. It is roughly the question 'Was there a set of contemporary and earlier events and relationships from which, together with the actual laws of nature and the dispositional properties of Caesar, it follows logically that Caesar will decide at a certain moment to cross the Rubicon?' It seems to me that the Predicate-in-Notion Principle leaves that question entirely open. It is therefore compatible with voluntary decisions not being completely determined causally by other *events within nature*.

On the other hand, it seems to me clear that Caesar's decision and every other event in his history was causally necessitated by God's decision to create a person of that kind and with that history in a world with such-and-such laws of physics and psychology. It was therefore determined by an event *outside nature*, viz. God's choice of a certain possible world and his creative actualization of that world. Leibniz wriggles a great deal on this point, but I cannot see that he can evade it.

4.4.1 Leibniz's views about freedom and determinism

The best account that Leibniz gave of his views is to be found in pp. 16–24 of Couturat's *Opuscules et fragments de Leibniz*.[1] The theory may be stated as follows.

Leibniz first distinguishes between metaphysical necessity and contingency. This we have already dealt with. It remains to consider what he meant by 'physical necessity'.

The behaviour of any actual body under given conditions is physically necessary, though metaphysically contingent. This means that its behaviour is entailed by the nature of the body and the circumstances in which it is placed and its past history together with the general laws of physics which hold in the actual world. But these laws are metaphysically contingent. They were freely willed by God because he saw that a world in which they hold would be better on the whole than one in which different laws held. It is, e.g., physically necessary that an unsupported body at rest near the earth's surface should fall to the ground if its specific gravity is greater than that of air; for this is entailed by the nature of actual bodies, and the law of gravitation, and the principle of Archimedes. But the law and the principle are metaphysically contingent; and so the fall of such a body, though physically necessary, is metaphysically contingent.

There is, however, one further qualification to be made. God may have decided, when he chose out a certain possible world and actualized

[1] [Morris and Parkinson, 96–105.]

it, that the law of gravitation should be suspended in a certain case, because he foresaw that it would be undesirable on the whole that a certain unsupported body should fall to the ground on a certain occasion. The body would then not fall, and we should call the event a 'miracle'. So we can say that physically necessary events are, in theory, predictable from a sufficient knowledge of the circumstances of the case and the laws of the actual world, provided only that God has not prearranged that the laws shall be miraculously suspended.

We come now to the voluntary actions of intelligent beings. Leibniz holds that they are determined, but are neither metaphysically nor physically necessary. We will now consider what he means by these statements.

(1) He holds as strongly as Spinoza that all talk of an undetermined event, in the sense of an event for which there is no sufficient reason, is nonsensical. The fact that a person will deliberately choose a certain action at a certain date is timelessly contained in the complete notion of him. God contemplated these voluntary actions first as mere possibilities, and then made his decision to actualize a certain world containing that person, in view of what he had foreseen. So the ultimate reason for the occurrence of any human action is the fact that a world containing a certain person who will act in a certain way on a certain occasion is, and was foreseen by God to be, on the whole better than any alternative possible world. The action is thus ultimately determined by God's decision to actualize that world. It is therefore not undetermined. God knows in *detail* the reasons for it, i.e. he knows how precisely a world which had not contained this person doing this action on this occasion would have been inferior on the whole to the actual world. We cannot know the reason in detail; we can only know in principle that there must be a reason and that it must be of that kind. I said that Leibniz and Spinoza agree that to talk of an undetermined event is nonsensical. Nevertheless, they meant very different things. Leibniz meant what I have just said. Spinoza meant that all events are metaphysically necessary.

(2) When Leibniz says that human voluntary actions are not even physically necessary he must, I think, mean the following. Even apart from the possibility of a miraculous suspension of the laws of psychology, it is theoretically impossible to predict with complete certainty what any man will choose in given circumstances, no matter how complete a knowledge one might have of all the other facts about him and of the laws of psychology.

If this is what he means, I think it is important and may well be true. Human minds have an individuality which, so far as we know, does not belong to bits of matter. There are certain laws which hold for *all* kinds of matter, viz. the laws of motion. Then again one can determine once and for all the characteristic dispositional properties of a particular kind of matter, e.g. copper, from a few samples of it, and then conclude that they are present in other samples which have not been tested. But the dispositional properties of a human being can be discovered only by observations made on *him*. Moreover they are liable to change in the course of a person's life in ways that cannot be predicted with any certainty. For these reasons the voluntary actions of a person could not be predicted, even in theory and barring miracles, with complete certainty from any conceivable extension of our knowledge of the laws of psychology, of his past history, and of his present circumstances.

It remains to notice some more special remarks which Leibniz makes on these topics:

(1) What does he mean by saying in the *Letters to Arnauld* that, in the case of contingent facts, 'reasons may incline without necessitating'?[1] In considering a proposition and the reasons for it there are two different questions to be raised. (a) Are the premisses necessary or contingent? (b) Is the connexion between the premisses and the conclusion demonstrative or merely confirmatory? In pure mathematics, e.g., the premisses are neccessary and the connexion is demonstrative. When a physician makes a diagnosis of a patient's disease from a knowledge of his symptoms and of roughly parallel cases in the past, the premisses are contingent and the connexion is merely confirmatory. Now, when Leibniz talks of cases where reasons incline but do not necessitate, I think he must mean, not only that the reasons are contingent, but also that they are insufficient to entail the conclusion but sufficient to give it a probability greater than one-half. If we apply this to the case of human voluntary decisions, it comes to the following. (a) If you know enough about a person's past history and present situation and the laws of human psychology, you can make very probable guesses as to how he will decide. But (b) however much your knowledge on these matters might be increased, it would be insufficient to enable you to make a prediction which would be absolutely certain barring miracles.

This interpretation seems to me to be supported by the following quotation from p. 21 of Couturat's *Fragments*.[2] Leibniz says there: 'It

---

[1] (G., II, 46. Mason, 50. Cf. G., II, 12. Mason, 5.]
[2] [Morris and Parkinson, 101.]

is not physically necessary that a man shall choose a certain alternative, however attractive and appreciably good it may seem to him, though there is an extremely strong presumption that he will do so.'

(2) Leibniz draws a distinction between men in this life, on the one hand, and angels and just men made perfect, on the other. He says that it is impossible that any person should choose what appears to him at the time to be the *worse* of two alternatives. But it is neither metaphysically nor physically necessary that a man in this life should choose what appears to him to be the *better* of two alternatives. He can often defer decision and turn his mind to other subjects, and it is impossible to be sure beforehand whether he will do so or not. This is not so with good angels and just men made perfect. It is physically necessary that they should always act virtuously, and therefore it would be theoretically possible to predict how they would decide on any occasion in which moral considerations entered, barring miracles.

(3) Leibniz believed that a great many of the states of any human mind are so feeble in intensity and so much like many other contemporary states of the same mind that they cannot be introspectively discriminated. Such states he calls 'unconscious perceptions'. He holds that the belief that there are undetermined decisions arises from the fact that we confine our search for the causes of our decisions to conscious mental states and ignore the existence and the causal efficacy of unconscious ones. Even if a decision is always completely determined by previous states, it is seldom or never completely determined by previous *conscious* states. So, if we confine our attention to conscious states and forget about unconscious ones, we shall be inclined to say that such a decision was not completely determined.

5 Principle of Sufficient Reason, contingency, and infinite complexity

There has been a good deal of controversy as to Leibniz's views on the relations between contingency, infinite complexity, and the Principle of Sufficient Reason. I will begin by collecting the most important of the views which Leibniz expressed on various occasions on this topic.

(1) All existential propositions, except the existence of God, are contingent. Leibniz accepted the Ontological Argument, and therefore held that the existence of God is contained in the notion of him. (2) A contingent proposition is true or false, as the case may be, in the actual world; but not in all possible worlds. Necessary propositions are true in all possible worlds. (3) Necessary propositions can be seen

directly to be analytic or they can be reduced to explicitly analytic propositions by a finite analysis. No contingent proposition can be made explicitly analytic, no matter how far the analysis of its terms may be carried. Leibniz says: 'Only God, who can comprehend the infinitely complex in one act, can see how the predicate is contained in the subject, and can understand *a priori* the reason for a contingent fact.'[1] Finite creatures have to learn such facts *a posteriori* by experience. Leibniz is also fond of comparing the analysis of a necessary fact to analysing an integer into a finite number of prime factors. And he compares the attempted analysis of a contingent fact to the attempt to approximate to a surd, like $\sqrt{2}$, by means of infinite series or infinite continued fractions, which at no stage are exactly equal to it. (4) The opposite of any necessary proposition involves a contradiction. We may therefore say that the Law of Contradiction is the principle on which all necessary propositions rest. The opposite of any contingent proposition is possible and involves no contradiction. Nevertheless there is a sufficient reason for the truth of every true contingent proposition. So we may say that contingent propositions depend on the Principle of Sufficient Reason. (5) Contingent propositions are dependent on God's will to actualize a certain one of the possible worlds. Necessary propositions are wholly independent of God's will. (6) There are universal contingent propositions as well as singular and particular ones. The actual laws of nature are universal but contingent. But Leibniz seems to have held that it is part of the notion of a world that there should be *some* general laws which hold in it.

5.1 Contingent facts and God's choice of the best

Let us consider an example which Leibniz discusses in his *Letters to Arnauld*, viz. Adam's act of disobedience in eating the apple. Leibniz has to hold that this is contained in the notion of the actual Adam; that it is nevertheless contingent; that it depends on God's will to create the actual Adam; and that it is nevertheless in a sense contrary to God's will.[2] I think that the essential points may be stated as follows.

It is possible in many different ways to make a selection out of the properties of the actual Adam which would suffice to distinguish him from all other *actual* individuals. Any such selection of properties constitutes a *sufficient description* of the actual Adam. If all superfluous

---

[1] [Couturat, 17. Morris and Parkinson, 97.]
[2] [G., II, 47–59. Loemker, 331–8.]

properties are left out of a *sufficient description* of the actual Adam we have a *minimal sufficient description* of him. Now anything that answered to any minimal sufficient description of the actual Adam might be called a 'possible Adam'.

Now it is quite certain that *some at least* of the minimal sufficient descriptions of the actual Adam, even if we put into them the actual laws of nature, do not contain or logically entail the property of disobeying God. E.g. we might sufficiently describe the actual Adam as a man without human parents. There is plainly no direct or indirect contradiction in the proposition 'The man without human parents did not disobey God.' In this sense we can say that there is a possible Adam who would have obeyed God. In general, the properties included in any minimal sufficient description of any actual individual could, without contradiction, be supplemented in innumerable different alternative ways. Any proposition, ascribing to an individual who answers to that description any predicate not contained in or entailed by that description, is contingent.

Suppose we take any minimal sufficient description of the actual Adam which does not include or logically entail the property of disobeying God. Then we can say that it depends on God's choice whether there should be anything answering to that description or not. And we can say that, if God should decide to actualize an individual answering to that description, it will still depend on God's choice whether that individual does or does not have the further property of disobeying God.

Now contrast this with the case of a kind of geometrical figure, e.g. the circle, on the supposition (which he would no doubt have assumed) that the axioms of Euclid are necessary propositions. *Any* property which is sufficient to distinguish the circle from other kinds of geometrical figures would, in combination with the axioms of Euclid, entail *all* the other geometrical properties common and peculiar to circles. Suppose we take any minimal sufficient description of the circle. No doubt it would have been open to God not to create anything answering to that description. But, *if* he did so and if the axioms of Euclid were necessary propositions, he could not help it having all the geometrical properties which are common and peculiar to circles.

We see then that there is good sense in saying that the truth of the contingent proposition that Adam disobeyed God is dependent on God's will, whilst the truth of the necessary proposition that $\sqrt{2}$ is irrational is independent of God's will. But it sounds paradoxical to say that God willed that Adam should disobey him, and that it was in

consequence of God's will that Adam was disobedient. These para-
doxes are, however, merely verbal. The solution is as follows.

According to Leibniz God contemplated all the various possible
worlds and actualized that one which would contain the greatest
balance of good over evil. Some of the possible worlds would have
contained an individual answering to any description of Adam which
we may take, and some would not. In some of the possible worlds
containing such an individual the complete notion of him would have
contained the predicate of disobeying God, in others it would have
contained the predicate of obeying God. Since the actual world contains an Adam who disobeyed God, God must have seen that that
possible world was better on the whole, in spite of this, than any which
contained no Adam or an obedient Adam. God foresaw the disobedience of the actual Adam and decided to actualize a world containing a disobedient Adam, because he saw that on the whole it was
better than any other possibility open to him. That is the sense in which
Adam's disobedience was a consequence of God's will.

We must distinguish, as Leibniz says, between God's *antecedent* and
his *consequent* volitions. God's antecedent volition was for an obedient
Adam, i.e. he would have preferred an obedient Adam to a disobedient one if he could have chosen simply between those two
alternatives. But he could not. He had to choose between a total state
of affairs containing a disobedient Adam, and other total states of
affairs containing no Adam or an obedient one. As he saw that the
former was *on the whole* better than any of the latter, his *consequent*
volition was for a disobedient Adam. E.g. without a fall there could
have been no redemption and perhaps no incarnation. And God may
have seen that the value of the redemption and the incarnation out-
weighed the disvalue of the fall.

5.2 Infinite complexity and contingency

There is admittedly some close connexion in Leibniz's mind between
infinite complexity, contingency, and the Principle of Sufficient Reason; but there is a difference of opinion among commentators as to
what precisely the connexion is. I will first give my own suggestion.

I think that Leibniz meant by the Principle of Sufficient Reason simply that there is a sufficient reason for the truth of *every* true proposition, whether necessary or contingent. In any particular case we
must distinguish (1) the general principle which is appealed to, and
(2) the detailed process of showing that the case falls under the principle.

In all necessary propositions the general principle which is appealed to is the Law of Contradiction. The detailed process consists in showing by means of analysis and deductive inference that the predicate is contained explicitly or implicitly in the definition or accepted description of the subject. In principle this could always be completed in a finite number of steps if the subject has a definition or accepted description. In all contingent propositions which are true the general principle which is appealed to is that God is perfectly wise and therefore never chooses capriciously and without a reason, and that he is perfectly good and therefore his governing motive is always to maximize the nett balance of good over evil. The detailed process would consist in showing how a world in which this contingent proposition is true would be better on the whole than any alternative possible world in which it would have been false.

The connexion of contingency with infinite complexity is easy to understand on this view. To know which world would be best on the whole we should have to consider all the states of all the substances in all the possible worlds at all moments, and to compare them with each other. It is plain that this would involve an infinitely extensive survey and an infinitely minute analysis, which no human being could possibly perform. So no one but God could know *in detail* the sufficient reason for the truth of any true contingent proposition. But we can know with complete certainty the general principle that there must be a sufficient reason for it, and that the sufficient reason must be of the kind which we have indicated.

I suspect that Leibniz sometimes used the phrase 'Principle of Sufficient Reason' to mean the *general* principle that there is a sufficient reason for the truth of *every* true proposition, and sometimes for the *special* principle which gives the sufficient reason for the truth of true *contingent* propositions. In the second sense it rests on the principle that God does not choose capriciously but always has a reason for what he does, and that his ultimate motive is always the desire to maximize the nett balance of good over evil. In the first sense it covers both this, as the sufficient reason for the truth of true *contingent* propositions, and the Law of Contradiction.

5.3 Contingency and actual existence

(1) There is a very important *epistemological* connexion between contingency and actual existence. In the case of an actual existent, one can learn, by one's own perception or by the reports of others, facts

about it which are not explicitly or implicitly contained in the description by which one distinguishes it from other existents. Thus I learn that the actual Adam disobeyed God from the report of the incident in the book of Genesis. Now this is the only way in which one can learn any contingent fact about an individual. This way is applicable only to individuals which can be or could have been perceived; and only actual existents can be perceived. It follows at once that the only contingent propositions which can be *known* are about actual existents. Any proposition which can be known about a merely possible existent must be one whose predicate is either explicitly or implicitly contained in the accepted description of that possible existent. It must therefore be necessary.

(2) Another point is this. If there were a contingent true proposition about a merely possible individual there could be no sufficient reason for it. The reason for its truth could not consist in the fact that the predicate is contained explicitly or implicitly in the definition or accepted description of the subject. For in that case the proposition would be necessary and not contingent. Again, the reason for its truth could not be that God had seen that a world in which this proposition was true would be on the whole better than any alternative world in which it would be false and had therefore decided to actualize that world. For by hypothesis God did *not* choose to actualize that world, but left it a mere possibility. So there would be no sufficient reason for the truth of any contingent proposition about a merely possible individual. If, then, we accept the principle that there is a sufficient reason for the truth of every true proposition, we must conclude that there *are* no contingent propositions about merely possible individuals. Every proposition about a merely possible individual is either necessary or impossible. This is what Leibniz held, and I think that this is the consistent view for him to take.

6 Denial of relations

I will begin by quoting two typical remarks by Leibniz on the topic of relations. Both occur in the *Letters to des Bosses*, but plenty of similar statements can be found elsewhere in his writings. (1) 'No accident can be at the same time in two or more subjects. . . Paternity in David is one thing and sonship in Solomon is another thing. But the common relationship is something merely mental, whose foundation is the modifications of the several terms.'[1] (2) 'The relations which connect

[1] [G., II, 486. Loemker, 609.]

two monads are not in either the one or the other, but equally in both at once; and therefore properly speaking in neither, but only in the mind. . . I do not think that you would wish to posit an accident which would inhere simultaneously in two subjects – one which, so to speak, has one leg in one and another leg in the other.'[1]

Leibniz's doctrine may be stated as follows. Undoubtedly there are *relational sentences* and we understand them; e.g. 'David was father of Solomon.' Again, there is a sense in which some such sentences express true propositions and others express false propositions. Cf., e.g., 'David was father of Solomon' and 'William III was father of Queen Anne'. But even a relational sentence which expresses a true proposition partly misrepresents the fact which makes it true. The sentence 'A has R to B' suggests that there is a single fact, composed of the two terms A and B and a peculiar kind of attribute R which joins them and is attached to both of them. This is misleading. If the relational sentence is true, it is made true by a conjunction of two facts, one entirely about A and the other entirely about B. The facts are of the form 'A has the quality q_1' and 'B has the quality q_2.' The relational form is a fiction imposed by the mind of the person who makes the relational judgment. Leibniz expresses this by saying that relations are only *phenomena*, but they are *phenomena bene fundata*. The foundations are those qualities in the two terms which are present when the relational judgment would commonly be said to be true, and absent when it would commonly be said to be false.

The following comments may be made on this. (1) I do not think that Leibniz has produced any real *argument* against the reality of relations. The idea of a relation just is the idea of an attribute with one leg in one term and another leg in another. To say that there cannot be such attributes is just a picturesque way of saying that there cannot be relations. So all that Leibniz really does is to ask us whether we do not find it self-evident, as he does, that all attributes must be pure qualities. If we do not, then he has nothing more to say.

(2) I think that both Leibniz and his opponents make the mistake of thinking of relationship in general by means of a picture drawn from one particular kind of relation. The picture is that of two bits of wood connected by a bit of string which is glued at one end to one of them and at the other end to the other. The string represents a relation, the bits of wood represent the terms, and the glue represents the inherence of the relation in each term. Such a picture is quite

---

[1] [G., II, 517. Cf. also Fifth Letter to Clarke in G., VII, 401. Loemker, 704. Alexander, 71.]

hopeless; for the string and the glue are *substances*, and not attributes, just as much as the bits of wood themselves. But criticisms on the defects of a certain very crude way of picturing the notion of relationships, and on the absurd implications which it has if taken literally, are not fatal to the notion itself.

(3) It seems to me that a true relational sentence expresses something genuine which would be left unexpressed if one merely made statements about the qualities of the terms. Take, e.g., the judgment '*A* is longer than *B*', where *A* and *B* are two bits of string. I suppose that the facts which Leibniz would call the foundations of the phenomenon would be, e.g., that *A* is so long and that *B* is so long. But these are plainly not equivalent to '*A* is longer than *B*'. Either we must add 'The length of *A* is greater than the length of *B*', or we must particularize and say e.g., '*A* is 2 inches long and *B* is 1 inch long.' On the first alternative, we have simply substituted a relational proposition about *lengths* for our original relational proposition about *bits of string*. On the second alternative we are reduced to relational propositions at the second move. For, in the first place, to say that '*A* is 2 inches long' involves stating a relationship between *A* and a standard rule. And, in the second place, we require the relational proposition that the number 2 is greater than the number 1. Moreover, it is plain that the two propositions about *A* alone and about *B* alone are in a certain sense more determinate than the proposition expressed by '*A* is longer than *B*.' The fact that *A* is longer than *B* does not entail that *A* is of any one determinate length or that *B* is of any one determinate length.

(4) I suspect that relations are thought to be fictions introduced by the mind of the observer for the following reason. It is particularly obvious that a good deal of preliminary mental and even bodily activity is often needed before one is in a position to make a relational judgment. To take a very simple case, it may be necessary to bring *A* and *B* together and lay them side by side with one end of each coinciding, before one can judge with certainty that *A* is longer than *B*. Such preliminary activity is not needed before making, e.g., the qualitative judgment '*A* is blue.' Now it is easy to think that the activities which are needed in order to *recognize* a relation in some sense *create the idea of a relation* and project it upon facts which are themselves non-relational. There is much less temptation to think this in the case of qualitative judgments. But there seems no reason to believe that this interpretation of the precedent mental activity as creative and projective and not merely revelatory is correct.

(5) I do not think that Leibniz ever makes much use of the *general* principle that *all* ostensibly relational facts are reducible to conjunctions of purely qualitative facts. What he really thinks important is a much more restricted principle which might be put as follows: 'There are no non-formal relations between *different substances*.' By 'formal relations' I mean such relations as similarity, identity, otherness, the subject–predicate relation, and so on. By 'non-formal relations' I mean such relations as spatial, temporal, and causal relations, and so on. (a) Leibniz assumes, e.g., that there is a plurality of substances which are similar in many fundamental respects, i.e. he accepts the formal relations of numerical diversity and similarity between different substances. (b) His theory of Pre-established Harmony, which we shall deal with later, presupposes that one can talk of certain states of different substances as being contemporary with each other. (c) His general account of simple substances presupposes that each total state of such a substance *precedes* some of its states and *follows* others of them, and that the successive states are causally interconnected. So the position is this. Leibniz makes assertions which, if they were valid at all, would be fatal to *all* relations. But in the rest of his system he presupposes the reality of formal relations between different substances; of temporal relations between total states of different monads; and of both temporal and causal relations between the various total states of each simple substance.

7 Identity of Indiscernibles

This is a famous principle of Leibniz's. He recognizes two kinds of difference, viz. numerical diversity or otherness, and qualitative dissimilarity or unlikeness. The principle is that whenever there is numerical diversity there must be qualitative dissimilarity; or, to put it quite simply, that there cannot be two individuals which are exactly alike in all their qualitative predicates. As McTaggart said, a better name for the principle would be 'The Dissimilarity of the Diverse'.

(1) In the *Letters to Arnauld* Leibniz asserts, but does not attempt to prove, that this follows from the Predicate-in-Notion Principle.[1] Does it really follow? Consider the following sentence: 'There might be two minds, A and B, whose dispositional properties were identical, whose histories occupied precisely the same period, and such that at each moment in the period the state of A was exactly like the contemporary

[1] [G., II, 42. Mason, 45.]

state of *B.*' I do not wish to assert positively that this sentence is significant. It might very well be alleged that, although it is unobjectionable in grammatical form, it does not present any proposition to the consideration of a person who utters or hears it. But I do assert the following two things. (a) The question whether the sentence is significant or not is quite independent of the Predicate-in-Notion Principle. (b) If the sentence does express a proposition, then the Predicate-in-Notion Principle does not refute it, unless we add the assumption that a substance is a complex whole composed of its predicates (or rather of the 'modifications' which correspond to its predicates) and containing no other constituent.

(2) The Identity of Indiscernibles plays an important part in the *Letters to Clarke*, where it is used in connexion with the controversy between the absolute and the relational theories of space, time and motion. It is very difficult to be sure which of the two following alternatives Leibniz means to assert: (a) That the very supposition that there might be two things exactly alike in their qualities is self-contradictory and meaningless. (b) That although the supposition is not logically impossible, we can be sure that God would not create two such things. As Clarke points out, Leibniz seems now to say one thing and now the other. E.g. in the Fourth Letter Leibniz says: 'to suppose two indiscernible things is to suppose the same thing under two names'.[1] This certainly suggests that he held that the alleged supposition, if taken literally, is self-contradictory and meaningless. If so, the principle is necessary. But elsewhere in this Letter, and still more explicitly in the Fifth Letter, he seems to take the other view. For instance, in the Fifth Letter he says that he does *not* maintain that it is absolutely impossible to suppose that there are two bodies which are exactly alike, but only that it would be contrary to God's wisdom to create two such bodies, and therefore we can be certain that there are not two such bodies.[2] This would seem to make the principle contingent.

I think that there are two things to be said about this apparent inconsistency. (a) There is certainly a sense in which it is possible to make, and to argue correctly and intelligibly from, a supposition which is, in another sense, impossible. That is precisely what happens, e.g., when one proves by *reductio ad absurdum* that there cannot be a rational fraction in its lowest terms whose square is equal to two. (b) Leibniz might merely be making a concession for the sake of argument when he seems to adopt the second alternative. His position might

[1] [G., VII, 372. Loemker, 687.]   [2] [G., VII, 394. Loemker, 699.]

perhaps be expressed as follows: 'I can see that the supposition that there might be two things exactly alike is self-contradictory. But, even if you will not grant me this, I can show that God never would create two such things and therefore that the supposition will always be false.'

(3) In the *Letters to Clarke* there is a close connexion between the Identity of Indiscernibles and the Principle of Sufficient Reason. The argument may be put as follows. Suppose, if that be an intelligible supposition, that there were two coexisting material particles A and B, exactly alike in all their qualities and dispositional properties. They would have to be in different places at every moment of their coexistence. Now for the present purpose it does not matter whether we assume the absolute or the relational theory of space. If P and Q are points of absolute space, there could be no possible reason for preferring to put A at P and B at Q rather than B at P and A at Q. But a similar consequence follows on the relational theory. In that case the point P is defined by certain spatial relations to a certain set of material particles taken as a system of reference, and the point Q is defined by certain other relations to the same set of particles. Now, if A and B are exactly alike in all their qualities and dispositional properties, there can be no possible reason for preferring to put A into the former relation and B into the latter rather than doing the opposite with them. If then God were to create two such particles, he would (a) be bound to put them in different places, and yet (b) would have no reason for choosing between the two alternatives which would arise by imagining the two particles being interchanged. Now God never acts without a sufficient reason. So we can conclude, either that the supposition is meaningless, or that, if it is not, God will never create two precisely similar particles and therefore there never will be two such particles.

Clarke was not satisfied with this.[1] He pointed out that a person might know that it would be much better to actualize *one or other* of two alternatives A and A' than to actualize *neither* of them, whilst at the same time he may see that it is a matter of complete indifference whether it should be A or A' that is actualized. On Leibniz's principle a person in this position would actualize *neither*, simply because he cannot actualize *both*, and has no reason to prefer one to the other; although he has a very good reason for preferring to actualize *one or other* of them to actualizing *neither*. Clarke says that in such a case of indifference a free agent chooses a certain one of the indifferent alternatives by a 'mere act of will'. Leibniz answers that, if this were possible,

[1] [G., VII, 381. Loemker, 691.]

which it is not, such motiveless choice would be indistinguishable from pure objective chance.[1] (I might remark that a man in this kind of situation would probably decide to associate the head of a coin with one of the alternatives and the tail with the other, to spin the coin, and to choose the alternative which he had associated with the side that should fall uppermost. But Leibniz would say that there must be some reason, however far-fetched, for his associating the head rather than the tail with the particular alternative with which he does decide to associate it. And in any case this expedient would not be open to God. For he would know beforehand how the coin would fall. So he would already be deciding on a certain alternative when he associated it with the face which he foresaw would fall uppermost.)

In any case these arguments in the *Letters to Clarke* would at most prove that there cannot be two coexistent *material particles* which are exactly alike. I do not see that they could refute my supposition about two coexisting minds which were exactly alike, if it be admitted that that supposition is intelligible.

(4) I think that there would be the following connexion between the Identity of Indiscernibles and Leibniz's doctrine about relations being *phenomena bene fundata*. Suppose it were true in the phenomenal sense that A stands in the relation R to B, where R is an asymmetrical relation, such as *earlier than* or *to the right of*. According to Leibniz the facts corresponding to this must be a conjunction of two purely qualitative facts of the form 'A has the quality q_1' and 'B has the quality q_2'. Now if the relation is asymmetrical q_1 and q_2 must plainly be different qualities. So we could say that it follows from Leibniz's view of relations that any two substances which, phenomenally speaking, stand in any asymmetrical relation to each other must differ in the qualities which are the foundation of that phenomenon, however much they may be alike in every other respect. If one could add the premiss that any two substances must, phenomenally speaking, stand in some asymmetrical relation to each other the Identity of Indiscernibles would follow. But I do not think that there is any reason to admit this premiss.

(5) Sometimes Leibniz appeals to the empirical fact that, however much alike two things may seem at first sight, you will always find qualitative differences between them if you look more carefully, use a microscope, etc. The argument would be that every increase in our powers of discrimination discloses qualitative differences in things which seemed exactly alike at the previous stage. Hence we may con-

[1] [G., VII, 390. Loemker, 697.]

clude that all cases of plurality of apparently exactly similar things are really cases of dissimilarity concealed by our imperfect powers of discrimination. This, I think, can be meant only as a popular illustration, or as a way of removing an apparent conflict between the Principle and observed facts. Leibniz would not expect to *prove* a fundamental metaphysical principle by empirical arguments.

8 The Principle of continuity

Russell points out that Leibniz asserted three kinds of continuity, viz. spatio-temporal continuity, continuity of cases, and continuity of kinds of actual substance.[1] Leibniz did not regard any of these kinds of continuity as metaphysically necessary. He seems to have thought that a breach of any of them would be either an aesthetic defect or would mean that less had been created where more might have been without any compensating disadvantage. Now Leibniz thought that mere quantity of existence, other things being equal, is a positive good. Therefore a breach of any of these kinds of continuity would be inconsistent with the wisdom or the goodness of God. He speaks of them as 'principles of the order of things'.

(1) The principle of spatio-temporal continuity rules out such possibilities as that a body should occupy a certain position at a certain moment and a certain other position at a certain later moment without occupying successively during the intervening period a continuous series of intermediate positions. Leibniz says in his *Letters to de Volder* that God *could* transcreate a body from one place to a remote place without its moving from the one to the other through a continuous series of intermediate positions.[2] I suppose that God could do this either instantaneously or after a lapse of time during which the body ceased to exist. But experience shows that he does not in fact do this, and it would conflict with 'the law of order' if he were to do so. (Since Leibniz's time there is some empirical evidence which can be interpreted to mean that electrons sometimes jump instantaneously from one orbit to another which is discontinuous with it.) Leibniz says explicitly that any objection which there is to discontinuity in changes of *place* applies equally to discontinuity in changes of *state*. He uses this principle in dynamics in his theory of the impact of bodies.

(2) Leibniz develops and applies continuity of *cases* in geometry

[1] [Russell, Section 27.]
[2] [G., II, 168. Loemker, 515–16.]

and particularly in dynamics. He puts the principle as follows. 'If two cases or data continuously approach each other, so that at length one passes into the other, the same must be true of their consequences.' He says that this depends on a more ultimate principle, viz. 'If the data are ordered, the *quaesita* must be ordered also' (*Principium quoddam generale.* G. M. [VI], 129).[1] Thus a circle can be regarded as a special case of an ellipse where the two axes have become equal. Rest can be regarded as infinitely slow motion. Equality can be regarded as infinitesimally small differences. By using these criteria Leibniz made an annihilating criticism of Descartes's proposed laws of the impact of bodies of various masses and with various velocities. He showed that they do not answer to these criteria.

Leibniz admits that in *composite* bodies a small change in the conditions can make a great change in the effects. (Cf., e.g., a stone on the edge of a precipice or a spark in gunpowder.) But there is no doubt that his principle is of very wide application and of great utility.

(3) Continuity of *kinds of actual substance* is used to show that every kind of substance whose existence is compatible with the laws of the actual world will in fact exist. According to Leibniz, the real quality which underlies the phenomenon of spatial position is something which he calls 'point of view'. Now the determinates under this determinable form a continuous three-dimensional aggregate. It would have been possible for God to have omitted to create substances with certain of these determinate qualities. If so we should have had the phenomenon of empty spaces within the world of matter. But we can be sure that God has created a substance for every point of view which is compatible with the general scheme of spatial relations which he laid down for the actual world. Therefore, phenomenally speaking, space is everywhere filled with matter. Again there is a continuous range of possible degrees of clearness and confusion in the cognitive powers of any mind. We can be sure that God has created a mind with every possible degree of clearness and confusion from the lowest to the highest limit.

---

[1] [The Latin sentence reads 'Datis nimirum ordinatis etiam quaesita esse ordinata.' Perhaps one might translate it as follows. 'As the data are ordered, so the solutions one is looking for must be ordered also.' There is a French version of the paper in G., III, 51–5, and an English translation of that version in Loemker, 351–4. In the French version of the paper the sentence reads 'Datis ordinatis etiam quaesita sunt ordinata.' Cf. also Couturat, 544.]

9 Denial of transeunt causation[1]

Leibniz held that it is impossible for two created substances to interact with each other. This is one of his most characteristic general principles. We must now consider his reasons.

(1) In the *Letters to Arnauld* he explicitly says that this is one of the many important consequences of the Predicate-in-Notion Principle.[2] But he does not explain in detail how it follows from that principle. In discussing this question we must bear in mind the following two facts.

(a) Leibniz never denied or doubted that certain kinds of state in one substance are accompanied or immediately followed by certain kinds of state in other substances in accordance with general rules. As we shall see later, he put forward the hypothesis of Pre-established Harmony in order to account for this fact. Now many people nowadays would say that this is all that transeunt causation means, and therefore that it must be consistent with the Predicate-in-Notion Principle if that principle is true. It is plain that Leibniz, like all his contemporaries, neither accepted nor even contemplated this analysis of causation. It is therefore futile to discuss the question on the assumption that he would have done so.

(b) This is reinforced by the fact that Leibniz held that there is *immanent* causation, i.e. that a state of a substance genuinely causes its immediate successor and is genuinely caused by its immediate predecessor. Since we have regularities of sequence both as regards states of different substances and as regards states of the same substance, and since Leibniz denies causation in the former case and asserts it in the latter, it is plain that he cannot have identified causation with regular sequence. He must have thought that there is something in the notion of *transeunt* causation which is incompatible with the Predicate-in-Notion Principle, but that there is nothing in the notion of *immanent* causation to conflict with it. Why should he have thought this?

I should guess that his mind may have moved somewhat as follows. He would hold that genuine transeunt causation involves *constraint* or

---

[1] [As was common at the time, Broad uses the spelling 'transeunt' when the word has this particular meaning, rather than 'transient', which is perhaps more common at present. For a discussion of the distinction between immanent and transeunt causation cf., e.g., W. E. Johnson, *Logic*, Part III (Cambridge, 1924), Chapter 9.]

[2] [G., II, 70. Mason, 85.]

interference exercised by one substance on the natural course of development of another. The two most obvious instances of ostensible transeunt action are the following: (i) when a body which, if left to itself would have remained at rest or would have continued to move with constant velocity in a certain straight line, is set in motion or is forced to move differently either by the impact of another moving body or by the pressure or tension of a constraining body, like a rail or a string, and (ii) when a person who, if left to his own devices, would have remained idle or would have acted in a certain way to please himself, is set at work or compelled to act in a different way by the commands or threats of another. The notion of immanent causation is bound up with the notion of how the history of a substance would have developed if it had been left to itself. The notion of transeunt causation is bound up with the notion of modifications imposed on that natural course of development by the interference of other substances; either continuously, as in the case of fixed constraints in dynamics, or sporadically, as in the case of occasional impacts or occasional threats.

Now I suspect that Leibniz would have argued as follows. Every fact about the occurrence of any state of a substance at any moment in its history subsists timelessly. Each substance is provided from the beginning with a special persistent modification corresponding to each such fact about it. All that ever happens to it is the emergence of each such disposition from quiescence to activity at the appropriate moment, and its subsequent reversion from activity to quiescence. So there is no meaning in the suggestion that it is from time to time constrained to develop in a different way from that in which it would have developed if left to itself. Its actual development is prescribed in every detail by its own complete notion, and is therefore identical with its natural unconstrained development.

If this is Leibniz's argument, my comment would be as follows. The fact that every state of a substance is present in it from the first as a disposition does not preclude the possibility that some of its states will be in part determined by the action of other substances upon it. Suppose that the notion of S contains the fact that it will swerve to the left at moment *t*. Why should it not also contain the fact that this swerve will be imposed on it then by the impact of substance *S'* upon it? If so, of course, the notion of *S'* will contain a complementary fact. To put it generally, the doctrine that every fact about the state of a substance at any moment is timeless entails nothing about the *content* of such facts. In particular it entails nothing, positive or negative, about *causation*. It is compatible with some states being uncaused, with some

being caused purely immanently, and with others being caused trans-
euntly through the action of other substances. On either of these
alternatives there would be additional facts of a higher order, which
would be no less timeless and no less contained in the complete notion
of the substance.

(2) The denial of transeunt causation would presumably follow from
the denial of the metaphysical truth of relational propositions. For to
say that such-and-such an event in S causes such-and-such an event in
S' is certainly to make a relational statement. If Leibniz's theory is true
the facts that correspond to it must be a fact which is entirely about S
and another fact which is entirely about S'. It seems to me, however,
that, if this line of argument were used, it would apply to *immanent*
causation also. To say that the state s_1 of S causes the state s_2 of S is
also to make a relational statement, though it now concerns two
states of the same substance and not two different substances. If the
general argument about relations were sound, we should have to say
that this relational statement too can only be phenomenally true. The
facts corresponding to it would be a fact which is entirely about the
state s_1, and another fact which is entirely about s_2. This general argument would also have to be applied to the statement that God creates
and sustains finite substances. This too would have to correspond to a
conjunction of facts, one wholly about God and the other wholly
about the finite substances. But this is not at all what Leibniz wants.
He wants to deny *transeunt* causation between *finite* substances, and to
keep both *immanent* causation within each finite substance and *transeunt*
causation between God and finite substances.

(3) In many places Leibniz uses an argument which is independent
of his other general principles. In the *Letters to des Bosses*, e.g., he says
that interaction is *impossible* because we cannot conceive how it could
take place; and that it would be *superfluous*, even if it were possible,
because of the Predicate-in-Notion Principle.[1] This line of argument
is stated more fully in the *Monadology*. It runs as follows: 'Accidents
cannot separate themselves from substances nor go about outside
them... Thus ... no accident could come into ... [a substance][2] ...
from outside.'[3]

It seems to me that this, like the argument against relations in
general, is really valid only as against a certain very crude imaginative
picture. The picture is that when A interacts with B something which

[1] [G., II, 503. Loemker, 613.]
[2] [This insertion is Broad's.]
[3] [G., VI, 608. Loemker, 643.]

was a state of *A* leaves *A*, travels to *B* during a period in which it is not a state of anything, and then joins up and becomes a state of *B*. This might be a more or less plausible picture of what happens in some cases of transeunt causation, e.g. when a hot body heats up a cooler one by radiation or conduction and itself gets cooler. But it is *only* a picture even in such cases. And in many others it is not even a plausible picture, e.g. it would not cover the case of a spark causing a mixture of oxygen and hydrogen to explode.

(4) Another argument which is used in the *Monadology* runs as follows: 'There is no way of explaining how a monad could be altered in quantity or internally changed by any created thing. For it is impossible to change the place of anything in it, or to conceive any internal motion which could be produced, described, increased or diminished in it.'[1]

This argument presupposes that all substances have been proved to be monads, i.e. unextended mental substances. We shall have to consider the grounds for this later on. But the argument also presupposes that, if one substance could influence another substance at all, it could do so only by moving it as a whole or altering the existing motion of some part of it. I can see no reason to accept this. A mind can admittedly change its states as a result of previous changes in *itself*; e.g. a desire may cause experiences of active exertion and these may cause a feeling of tiredness. Why should it be impossible to suppose that some such change in one mind might be caused telepathically by the action of *another* mind?

[1] [G., VI, 608–9. Loemker, 643.]

3

LEIBNIZ'S THEORY OF CORPOREAL SUBSTANCES

I am going to use the technical term 'corporeal substance' instead of the ordinary term 'matter', because, as we shall see, Leibniz used 'matter' in a technical sense taken from the Scholastic philosophy, and in that sense even purely mental substances contain 'matter' as an essential factor.

1 Background of Leibniz's theories

Leibniz says in Section 11 of the *Discours* that at one time he shared the common view of contemporary 'advanced thinkers', i.e. of Descartes and his followers, of Hobbes, of Bacon, etc., that the Scholastic philosophy is futile.[1] But further reflexion forced him to recognize that it contains features which are essential to any sound philosophy. In his letter of 14 July 1686 to Arnauld he says that he has been driven back, against his will, to the Scholastic doctrine of *substantial forms*.[2] The Scholastic philosophy in general, and the doctrine of substantial forms in particular, would be perfectly familiar to Leibniz and all his educated contemporaries. But it is quite strange to most of us. I do not think that it is possible to understand Leibniz properly unless one knows something about the Scholastic doctrine of substance. So I shall begin with a short sketch of it.

1.1 Scholastic doctrine of substance

The fundamental concepts in the Scholastic philosophy are the correlated notions of *form* and *stuff*. (I shall use the word *stuff* to translate the technical term *materia;* to translate it as 'matter' is misleading nowadays.) Every body was regarded as involving the two factors of form and stuff. Thus, e.g., a man, a lion, and an oak-tree are ultimately composed of the same kind of stuff. Their characteristic differences arise from the different forms which inform different parcels of this common stuff.

[1] [G., IV, 435. Loemker, 309.]   [2] [G., II, 58. Loemker, 338.]

We notice two very different kinds of change in the external world. (1) In some cases we should say that the same substance has persisted and has merely changed its states. Thus a man is sometimes asleep and sometimes awake; a body is sometimes cold, sometimes hot, sometimes solid, and sometimes liquid; and so on. (2) In other cases we are inclined to say that a new substance has been generated or an old one destroyed. A typical example of the former is when a caterpillar changes into a moth or a tadpole into a frog. The most typical example of the latter is when an organism dies, and first ceases to perform its characteristic functions and then begins to rot and break up.

Now all changes in bodies were regarded as changes in form. It was held that the ultimate stuff (*materia prima*) can neither be generated nor destroyed in the course of nature. But the distinction between the two kinds of change led to a distinction between two kinds of form, viz. accidental and substantial. When a certain body continues to exist but changes, e.g. from being solid to being liquid, its stuff keeps the same substantial form and simply exchanges one accidental form for another. But, when an acorn becomes an oak-tree and a caterpillar becomes a moth, certain stuff acquires a new substantial form. This stuff, or more often other stuff which gradually replaces it, keeps this substantial form so long as this oak-tree or this moth continues to live. It imposes itself on and organizes the new stuff that is taken in the form of food and drink and air. It is capable within limits of restoring the organism to a normal state if it is injured. But gradually the organizing power of the substantial form over the stuff gets weaker. At length the stuff-constituent in the organism loses its substantial form and then the organism ceases to exist as an oak-tree or a moth. The stuff becomes the stuff of a corpse, which is not a single substance but is an aggregate of bodies of various kinds without any one substantial form to hold them together as a single living organism of a certain species.

It will be seen that the notion of substantial form applies most obviously to those bodies which are natural units, such as a living human body, a moth, or an oak-tree. It would not apply at all obviously to a lump of gold or a drop of water, though it might perhaps apply to a single crystal or atom of gold or a single crystal of ice or molecule of water. So the clearest instances of the notion are provided by men and the higher kinds of animal and vegetable organism.

The next point to notice is that many, though not all, Scholastics held that there can be and in fact are certain substances which are pure forms without stuff. Everyone held that God was such a substance, and the Thomists held that every angel is such a substance. On the other hand, no one held that there could be stuff completely devoid of form. The notion of *materia prima* was regarded as a factor incapable of actual separate existence.

Now, according to the Thomists at any rate, a human soul is in a very peculiar position. It is a substantial form, but it is not by itself a substance, as an angelic form is. Its nature is to inform a certain living body of a characteristic kind, viz. that of a certain individual man. But it is capable of existing in a kind of anomalous state during long intervals in separation from any kind of stuff. That is what happens to a human soul between the death of its body and the Day of Judgment, when it is once more reunited with an appropriate human body. The substantial form of a non-rational animal or a plant, on the other hand, was not generally supposed to exist when it is not actually informing the stuff of a living cat or oak-tree or whatever it may be.

So there are at least three kinds of substantial form, which can be arranged in a hierarchy as follows. (1) Forms which suffice by themselves, without any stuff, to constitute a substance. According to the Thomists, each angel is an instance of such a form. (2) Forms which are capable of existing temporarily and in a kind of dormant state without informing any stuff, but which do not suffice without stuff to constitute a substance. When such a form informs the stuff appropriate to it the two together constitute a substance which is a genuine individual unit. According to the Thomists human souls are such forms. A substance composed of such a form and the stuff which it informs is a particular human individual, e.g. the man John Smith. (3) Forms which were generally held to be incapable of existing even temporarily unless they are informing stuff of an appropriate kind. When such a form informs the stuff which is appropriate to it the two together make up a substance which is a genuine individual of a certain species, e.g. a cat or an oak-tree or (perhaps) a crystal of gold.

The functions of a substantial form are therefore two-fold. (1) It is because of its presence in certain stuff that there is a substance of a *certain specific kind*, e.g. a man or a cat or an oak-tree. (2) It is because of its continued presence that a substance is and remains a single persistent *natural unit*, in spite of having a plurality of contemporary parts, in spite of continual gradual changes of stuff, and in spite of occasional sudden changes of stuff due to accidents and injuries.

1.2 The Cartesian view

We must next consider the Cartesian view. This was a reaction against the Scholastic theory. It was based partly on the new scientific methods and discoveries of men like Galileo; partly on a reversion to Platonic and Augustinian philosophy, as opposed to the Aristotelian philosophy of which Thomism was a development; and partly on Descartes's own mathematical, scientific and philosophical discoveries. For the present purpose the essential points are the following.

(1) Of the three kinds of substantial forms Descartes rejected all but the first. He held that each human soul is a pure form without stuff, capable of a full existence without a body, and in fact very much like an angel as conceived by the Thomists. He denied that irrational animals and plants have substantial forms. They are completely devoid of consciousness, and are just extremely complicated natural machines. All their physiological and their biological characteristics can be and should be fully accounted for mechanically in terms of their structure and the general laws of motion.

(2) A human soul, though it is a kind of substantial form, is not the form of its body in the sense in which the Scholastics believed. A human body is as much a machine as the body of an irrational animal or a plant. All its physiological and biological characteristics are to be accounted for mechanically. But there is a temporary and very mysterious connexion, which lasts for a longer or shorter period, between each living human body and a certain human soul. Certain processes in a human body produce sensations, images and emotions in the soul which is attached to it; and volitions in a human soul produce certain effects in the body to which it is attached. These effects are very strictly limited. In the first place, there is only one point in a human body at which the soul which is attached to it can affect it, viz. a certain part of the brain called the 'pineal gland'. Secondly, the only effect which it can produce is to alter the *direction* of a current of fluid called 'animal spirits' which circulates in the nerves and the cavities in the brain. Descartes thought he could prove from the perfection of God that the total quantity of motion in the corporeal universe as a whole cannot be changed. So the only effect that a soul can have is to make changes in the *direction* of certain already existing motions, without increasing or diminishing the *amount*. (The action might be compared to that of a pointsman who shunts a train into this, that, or the other branch.) The remote consequences of these actions of a soul on the pineal gland of the body with which it is connected are rational speech and planned action by that

body. It is obvious that Descartes's views on this point are very unsatisfactory and that his position was unstable. It had already been severely attacked by the Occasionalists and others when Leibniz began to write.

(3) Descartes held that the only essential properties of any corporeal substance are geometrical and kinematic, i.e. shape, size, position, and motion-or-rest. He held that colour, temperature, taste, smell, etc. are mind-dependent and do not belong to bodies themselves but are, so to speak, projected into them by the observer. But, if he is to be taken literally, he went further than this. If the only essential properties of corporeal substances are geometrical and kinematic, then they have no dynamical properties, such as mass, force, energy, etc. These also must be projected into them by the observer. In effect Descartes seems to have identified the *materia prima* of the Scholastics with an infinitely extended, perfectly homogeneous, continuous, incompressible fluid, with no qualities of its own. It is differentiated only by there being various currents and whirlpools in various parts of it. Particular bodies are parts of this fluid marked out from the surrounding fluid by particular kinds of motion. So it might be said that the stuff of all bodies is this universal fluid, and that the form of any particular body is the mode of motion which marks out one part of the fluid from its surroundings.

(4) Although Descartes spoke of human souls and of all kinds of bodies as 'substances', he held that there is an important sense of the word in which these can be called 'substances' only by courtesy. In this sense the only genuine substance is God. The point is this. He held that it is a mistake to think that a mind or a body is first created by God, and thereafter continues to exist and to pursue its adventures without any further action on God's part. He thinks that unless God actively intervened at every moment to maintain it, any created thing would at once cease to exist. A created thing persists only in so far as God continually re-creates it from moment to moment. God is the only existent which does not need to be kept in existence from outside itself, and in that sense he is the only genuine substance. A human soul or an atom would count as a substance, in contrast, e.g., to a particular experience or a particular volition, in so far as it depends on *nothing but* the creative action of God for its continued existence. A particular experience depends primarily on the soul in which it occurs, and secondarily on God who creates and sustains that soul. Therefore it is not a substance even by courtesy. By Leibniz's time this doctrine had been worked out to very startling consequences, in one direction by the Occasionalists culminating in Malebranche, and in another direction by Spinoza.

1.3 Leibniz's general reaction to Scholasticism and Cartesianism

Leibniz accepted much in the new scientific outlook and in the philosophic basis which Descartes had tried to provide for it. He also made very important contributions to mathematics and dynamics. He states explicitly again and again that every particular phenomenon in the corporeal world (including physiological and biological phenomena) must be explained mechanically. He held that there is a certain general principle in dynamics, viz. what we should call the 'Conservation of Momentum', which rules out even the small amount of action of souls on bodies which Descartes had admitted. He wholly agrees with the Cartesians that it is useless to appeal, as the Scholastics did, to substantial forms in order to explain scientifically any particular natural phenomenon. He agrees also with them, and with nearly all the leading scientists and philosophers of his day, in holding that colour, temperature, etc. do not belong to corporeal substances as such, but are in some sense projected into them by the mind of the observer. He agrees also that the external world is a plenum, with no empty volumes within it, and no empty region surrounding it.

But here his agreement ends. He holds that the doctrine that corporeal substance has nothing but geometrical and kinematic properties is both internally inconsistent and impossible to reconcile with the facts of dynamics. He holds that the laws of motion involve in the last resort something which is not merely geometric or kinematic, viz. the notion of *force*; and that force implies something like the Scholastic substantial form. He thinks that we are led to substantial forms also by considering the implications of the endless divisibility of corporeal substance. Lastly, he thinks that the Predicate-in-Notion Principle leads to the same conclusion.

We will now consider his arguments. In doing so we must remember that he might be perfectly successful in the negative part, i.e. in showing that the Cartesian account of corporeal substance is untenable, but the following question would still remain: is it either (a) necessary or (b) sufficient to postulate substantial forms in order to give a satisfactory account of corporeal substance?

2 Extension and motion

Leibniz argues that extension is not a simple unanalysable characteristic, and that it could not possibly be an adequate account of anything

THEORY OF CORPOREAL SUBSTANCES 55

to say that it had such-and-such a shape, size, position, and motion. His arguments are as follows.

(1) The notion of spatial extension is analysable. It has something in common with duration, viz. the factor of continuous repetition or diffusion. Taking bodies as they appear to the senses, their extension seems to consist in the continuous diffusion of some sensible quality, e.g. whiteness in the case of milk, over an area or throughout a volume. In spatial extension we have continuous diffusion of what is *coexistent*, in duration we have continuous diffusion of what is *successive*. Thus the notion of an extended object essentially involves the notion of some *non-geometrical* quality which is diffused continuously and simultaneously. Of course Leibniz would not admit that the quality could really be a colour, such as whiteness in milk, because he agrees with the Cartesians that colours are qualities which the observer projects into the things which he perceives. But there must be some real extensible quality in extended objects which *really* is continuously and simultaneously different, as whiteness *appears* to be to a person who looks at a glass of milk or a white cloud.

I think it is plain that Leibniz is right here. To talk of anything being *merely* extended, without any extensible quality which fills and marks out its area or volume is to talk nonsense. I would add, however, that there is something peculiar and unanalysable in the notion of extension, viz. the factor of *spatial* diffusion. This may be *analogous* to temporal diffusion in the case of duration, and to the discontinuous simultaneous repetition which is at the basis of number according to Leibniz. But it has its own unique character. It would be misleading to say simply that the notion of extension can be analysed into the notions of plurality, continuity, and simultaneity, and that the notion of duration can be analysed into those of plurality, continuity, and succession. What is peculiar to extension is the unique way in which an extensible quality constitutes a continuous diffused whole of coexistent adjoined parts.

(2) Not only is extension meaningless unless the notion of extensible qualities is introduced, to talk of *motion* in a completely homogeneous continuous fluid is also to talk without thinking. For just try to consider what would happen. A portion of the fluid would move out of a certain region and would continuously be replaced by other portions of the fluid. The motion would of course be circulatory. Now that which flowed into any region would be exactly like that which flowed out of it. There would have been a change only in name. We disguise from ourselves the fact that what we are saying is meaningless

by imagining this portion as somehow marked off from the rest by being contained in a kind of infinitely thin flexible skin, distinguished by its colour or some other sensible quality from its surroundings. But this is to deny tacitly what we are asserting explicitly, viz. that the fluid is completely homogeneous and has nothing but geometrical and kinematic properties. This argument would hold even if motion were something absolute; but we shall see shortly that Leibniz held it to be merely a change of relationships, and therefore, on his general principles, at best a *phenomenon bene fundatum.*

Leibniz concludes, quite rightly I think, from these two arguments, that what Descartes calls 'extension', i.e. purely geometrical and kinematic properties, is an essentially incomplete notion which could not conceivably suffice by itself to constitute the whole essence of anything.

3 Relativity of space, time and motion

It will be as well to consider Leibniz's doctrine of the relativity of space, time, and motion here. It is most clearly stated in the *Letters to Clarke.* Newton had definitely asserted in the *Principia* that Dynamics requires one to postulate absolute space, time, and motion; and Clarke represented Newton in this controversy.

In order to understand the controversy we must begin by stating Newton's view, as it emerged in Clarke's letters. It may be summarized as follows. (1) Space is logically prior to matter, and Time is logically prior to events and processes. (2) The volume of a body is a property of it, but the space which it occupies is not. A limited region of space which happens to be occupied by a body is a part of the one unlimited Space. Even if the whole of infinite Space were occupied by corporeal substance, still Space would not be a property of that infinite body. The infinite body would still be merely *in* Space, as finite bodies are in various parts of Space. The same remarks apply *mutatis mutandis* to Time and events or processes. (3) Strictly speaking, Space is indivisible. It is meaningless to suggest that the regions of Space which are adjoined might be separated. It is also meaningless to suggest that there might be holes in Space. Similar remarks apply *mutatis mutandis* to Time. (4) Space is actually, and not just potentially, infinite in every direction. Time had no beginning and will have no end. (5) Since Time is logically prior to the events and process which happen to occupy it, it is intelligible to suggest that the universe might have been created at an earlier or later moment than that at which it was in fact created. Again, since Space is logically prior to the things and events which happen to occupy it, both the two following suggestions are intelligible on the supposition that the corporeal universe is of finite extent. (a) That, without any difference in its internal structure, it *might have been* created in a different region of Space. (b) That it might at any moment *be moved* as a whole by God from one part of Space to another, or be given an absolute rotation about any direction in Space. If this rectilinear motion were non-uniform, or if the universe were subjected to an absolute rotation, these absolute motions would betray themselves by observable forces within the world. Otherwise, they would remain unobservable. (6) Absolute motion involves absolute Space and absolute Time. Its distinction from relative motion is evidenced by the existence of centrifugal forces, by the flattening of the earth at the poles, and so on. (7) A region of Space or a stretch of Time has an absolute magnitude. Different regions can be compared in respect of their absolute volume, and different stretches in respect of their absolute duration. (8) God does not exist in Space and Time in the sense in which created things and events do so. But he is immediately present to every part of unbounded Space throughout the whole of unending Time. In this way he is continually aware of all created things, and he acts upon them, but they do not react upon him.

Leibniz's argument against the absolute theory rests on the Principle of Sufficient Reason and the Identity of Indiscernibles. It may be summarized as follows. Let us grant for the sake of argument that the Absolute Theory is in some sense an intelligible hypothesis and not just meaningless verbiage. If the theory were true, the created universe could have occupied, without being in any way different internally, a different stretch of time or a different region of space. Now there would have been no possible reason for preferring to put it in one stretch of time or one region of space rather than another. Therefore God, who never makes a choice without a sufficient reason, would not have created a universe at all. But, since there is a universe, we know that he has created one. Therefore we can be certain that the Absolute Theory is false, even if it is not meaningless. If, on the other hand, the Relational Theory were true, these so-called alternative ways of locating the world in space or in time would not be genuine alternative possibilities. On the Relational Theory there is no actual space or time existing prior to the creation of things and events. God creates space in and through creating bodies and arranging them spatially in relation to each other. And he creates time in and through creating events in temporal relations to each other.

It was not clear to Clarke, and it is not clear to me, whether Leibniz meant to go further and positively assert that the Absolute Theory is meaningless verbiage. In the Fifth Letter[1] he says explicitly that the supposition of the universe as a whole being moved is *meaningless*, because there could be no space outside it. In the same Letter he says that motion must be *in principle* observable. It need not be actually observed; but there is no motion where there is no change that *could be* observed, and there is no change where none *could be* observed.

These passages suggest that he held the more radical view that the Absolute Theory is meaningless verbiage. But I think that his statements are fairly susceptible of either of the two following interpretations. (1) The Absolute Theory, and the various questions which arise in connexion with it, are *intrinsically* meaningless. (2) Even though the Absolute Theory and the questions which arise in connexion with it be *not intrinsically* meaningless, yet we can reject it and accept the Relational Theory because of the argument founded on the Principle of Sufficient Reason. And in *terms of the Relational Theory* these questions *are* meaningless. I suspect that Leibniz himself held the first view, but contented himself with the second for controversial purposes.

Is the argument based on the Principle of Sufficient Reason valid relatively to its own premisses? It seems to me that, if we suppose that God existed and had a series of experiences before he created the world, he might have perfectly good reasons for creating it when the series of his own experiences had reached a certain stage of development rather than before or afterwards. Suppose it is intelligible to talk of absolute time. Then God might have a perfectly good reason for creating the world at a certain moment of absolute time. The reason could be, not in anything special in that moment itself, but in the stage of development reached by his own experiences at that moment. I do not think that a similar argument could be used to show that God might have a good *internal* reason for creating the world in one region of Absolute Space rather than another. And I am pretty sure that Leibniz would have rejected the premiss of my argument about time. He would have denied that God has successive experiences as created minds do.

Leibniz's own account of the Relational Theory of Space occurs in the Fifth Letter.[2] It may be summarized as follows. Suppose that certain bodies X, Y, Z, . . . do not change their mutual spatial relations during a certain interval. Suppose further that, if there is a change during this interval in their spatial relations to certain other bodies, the

[1] [G., VII, 389–420. Loemker, 696–717.]   [2] [ibid.]

cause of it has not been in themselves. Then we can say that the bodies of X, Y, Z, . . . have constituted a 'rigid fixed system' during the interval in question. Suppose that, at some moment within this interval, a certain body A stood in certain spatial relations to the bodies of this system. Suppose that at a later moment within the interval A ceased to stand in these relations to them. And suppose, at some later moment within the interval, another body B began to stand to those bodies in precisely similar relations to those in which A had formerly stood. Then we can say that 'B has come to *occupy the same place as* A formerly occupied.' If and only if the causes of these changes of relative position have been in A and in B respectively, we can say that A and B have 'been in motion'. Leibniz then defines 'a place' in terms of the relation of 'occupying the same place'. Finally he defines 'space' as the collection of all simultaneous places.

Speaking in contemporary terminology, we may say that Leibniz regards Space as a logical construction out of places, and he regards a place as a logical construction out of facts about the spatial relations of bodies. And he holds that the notion of Absolute Space and absolute places is a fallacy of misplaced concreteness.

Leibniz sometimes argues in the *Letters to Clarke* that the Relational Theory of Space entails that there can be no empty spaces within the world, and that there cannot be empty space outside the world. In the Fifth Letter, e.g., he says: 'Since space in itself is an ideal thing . . . space outside the world must needs be imaginary. . . The case is the same with empty space within the world, which I take also to be imaginary.'[1] His more usual view, which also occurs in the *Letters to Clarke*, is that God *could* have limited the quantity of corporeal substance, but that it is very *unlikely* that a perfectly wise and benevolent creator would have done so.

The more radical view is quite certainly mistaken. Of course, if the Absolute Theory is false, space does not exist, in the sense in which the Newtonians thought it did, either outside the world, if that be finite, or inside the receiver of an air-pump if that could be completely exhausted. But it is quite easy to state, in terms of the Relational Theory, any of the following hypotheses: (1) That the world is of finite extent. (2) That, if it is of finite extent, it *might have been* bigger or smaller at a given moment than it in fact was then. (3) That it might *become* bigger or smaller in future than it now is. I will now proceed to show how this can be done.

Suppose you take as unit distance the distance at a given moment

[1] [G., VII, 396. Loemker, 701.]

between two particles P and Q. Then to say that the universe is of finite extent is to say that there is a finite integer N such that the distance between any two actual particles is less than N times the distance between P and Q. To say that it might have been bigger or smaller at a certain moment than it in fact was then, is to say that it is logically possible that N might have been bigger or smaller than it in fact was then. To say that there might be an empty hole within the world is to say that there might be pairs of particles at a finite distance apart which have no particle between them, and that the aggregate of such particles might be so arranged as to form a closed surface.

There is one other point of some importance. It is clear that the controversy between Leibniz and Clarke is conducted at what Leibniz would regard as an intermediate level of philosophical rigour and thoroughness. It is indeed a philosophical, and not merely a scientific, discussion. But Leibniz is granting for the sake of argument certain assumptions which he would claim to have refuted elsewhere. He is granting the reality of relations; but, as we know, he holds that relations between different substances are at best *phenomena bene fundata*. So the relational theory of space, time, and motion, though far nearer the truth than Newton's absolute theory, must itself be only an approximation to the truth. Suppose we say that body A is in such-and-such spatial relation to body B and that these relations are changing at such-and-such a rate. And suppose that this statement would, in the ordinary sense, be called true. If Leibniz's general theory of relations is correct the truth underlying it must be that A has a certain pure quality, that B has a certain other pure quality, and that one or other or both of these qualities are changing at a certain rate.

W. E. Johnson pointed out that there are two different distinctions involved in the controversy between the absolute and the relative theories of space.[1] (Similar remarks apply to time also, but we will ignore it.) (1) Is spatial position a pure quality or a relational property? (2) On either alternative is it a quality of or a relation between material particles *directly*? Or does it belong primarily to particular existents of a peculiar kind, viz. points or regions of a peculiar entity called 'Space', and only in a derivative sense to material particles in virtue of their occupying points or regions of Space? This question might be put in the form: Is space substantival or adjectival in character? Newton held both that space is substantival and that spatial position is a pure quality. Leibniz in the *Letters to Clarke* argues that space is adjectival; that spatial position is a relational property; and that the spatial relations

[1] [W. E. Johnson, *Logic*, Part II (Cambridge, 1922), 165ff.]

between material particles are *direct* and not derived from the facts
that they occupy points of space and that these are spatially related in
the primary sense. But ultimately Leibniz must hold what Johnson
would call a form of the adjectival qualitative theory. The real basis
of the phenomenon of spatial position must be certain pure qualities
in the substances which we perceive as bodies. Later on we shall see
that these qualities are what Leibniz calls the 'points of view' of
monads.

4 Dynamical properties of bodies[1]

It still remains to identify the objective non-geometrical extensible
quality, whose continuous simultaneous diffusion constitutes the extension of an extended object. Leibniz thinks that reflexion on the
dynamical properties of bodies enables us to identify this quality, and
at the same time to reinforce the view that the essence of corporeal
substances cannot be extension.

4.1 Impenetrability

We want to find an extensible quality which, like extension, is common to all bodies under all conditions, e.g. whether they are solid,
liquid or gaseous. Leibniz suggests that this characteristic is *impenetrability*. In so far as a body is considered as an extended object it is conceived as characterized by impenetrability diffused throughout a
certain volume or over a certain closed surface.

This property of impenetrability (or *antitypia* as Leibniz often calls
it) needs a little explanation. It may be defined as the fact that two
bodies cannot at the same time *continuously* occupy the same region.
You might say that this is obvious enough when both are hard solids.
But what about a solution of sugar in water, or a mixture of water and
wine, or a mixture of air and ammonia? The answer which is always
given is the following.

The volume is not *continuously* occupied either by water or by wine.
Each body consists of a vast number of very small particles with very
small spaces between them, and the particles of the one body are in the
spaces between those of the other body. No particle of water ever
occupies the same place as any particle of wine. You might compare
the sense in which the mixture occupies the containing vessel to that
in which Trafalgar Square might be simultaneously occupied by a

[1] [G. M., VI, 234–54. Loemker, 435–50.]

crowd composed of white men and of Negroes interspersed. Even if it were held that the vessel is continuously occupied by the mixture as a whole, it would be only discontinuously occupied by each constituent of the mixture. This explanation shows that impenetrability has nothing whatever to do with hardness or softness. If the ultimate particles of liquids were themselves liquid, it would still be the case that no two of them could occupy the same place at the same time.

With this explanation we can understand that what Leibniz means is this. A necessary condition for saying that a certain volume is filled with corporeal substance at a certain moment is that no other corporeal substance can occupy any part of that volume unless and until it pushes before it or thrusts aside the present contents of that region.

4.2 Inertial quiescence

This condition, however, is not sufficient. A body might be impenetrable, i.e. it might be that no other body could occupy its place without first shifting it. But it is logically possible that it might offer no *resistance to being shifted*, i.e. it might be that another body could, without losing any of its own motion, push it forward or thrust it aside. It is another essential property of corporeal substance that this logical possibility is never realized. No body can be set in motion by the impact of another body without the latter losing some of its own motion in the process. I am going to call this property 'inertial quiescence'.

4.3 Inertial self-propagation

Extension, impenetrability, and inertial quiescence are still insufficient. It is logically possible that a body should need an external force, not only to *set* it in motion, but also to *keep* it moving. It might be that it would at once cease to move if the forces which had set it in motion ceased to act on it. Or, failing that, it might be that the velocity which it had acquired would gradually and automatically die away if no external force acted to keep it up. It is another essential property of corporeal substance that this logical possibility is not realized. If a body moves *into* a place with a certain speed and in a certain direction, it will at the same instant move *out of* that place with the *same* speed and in the *same* direction, unless it is then and there acted upon from outside. And any moving body which causes a change in the speed or the direction of motion of another body by colliding with it will suffer a change in its own motion by doing so. I am going to call this property 'inertial self-propagation'.

Before going further I will make the following comments. (1) Leibniz lumps together inertial quiescence and inertial self-propagation under the common name of 'inertia'. It seems to me important to distinguish them, since the former does not logically entail the latter. (2) Leibniz seems to me sometimes to talk as if impenetrability implied an infinite natural force of resistance to penetration. I think that this is a mistake. The impossibility of the same region being simultaneously and continuously occupied by two bodies seems to me to be a *logical* impossibility depending on our criteria for judging 'the same' and 'different' bodies. No one objects, e.g., to the same region being simultaneously and continuously occupied by an electric and a magnetic field. (3) Descartes was quite well aware of the facts of impenetrability and inertial quiescence and inertial self-propagation. But, since they *are* essential properties of bodies and they certainly *are not* logical consequences of their purely geometrical and kinematic properties, Leibniz was quite right to insist that they refute the doctrine that the essence of corporeal substance is extension.

4.4 Force

A. *Passive*. Leibniz classifies impenetrability and the two kinds of inertia together under the name of 'passive force'.[1] For reasons already given I do not think that impenetrability should be counted as force at all. It seems to me also that inertial self-propagation, as distinct from inertial quiescence, should be counted as something active and not as something merely passive.

He holds that the passive force in any body is everywhere the same, and that the total amount of it in a body is proportional to its volume. He admits, of course, that there is a sense in which one body, e.g. a sphere of lead, has greater mass and therefore greater inertia than another of the same size, e.g. an equal sphere of wood. But he says that this is because each of these bodies is porous, like a sponge, or is a disconnected collection, like a cloud. The lead is much less porous than the wood, and so the quantity of lead-material in a sphere of lead is much greater than the quantity of wood-material in an equal sphere of wood. But I understand him to hold that, if two equal volumes are *continuously* occupied by corporeal substance, the mass of each would be the same. I do not think that he produces any good reason for this.

[1] [G. M., VI, 236–7. Loemker, 437.]

B. *Active*. Besides the properties already mentioned bodies have dynamic properties. Any body which is in motion is capable of producing effects on other bodies. Its power of doing this is greater the more massive it is and the faster it is moving. Again, a body which is raised up, e.g. the weight of a clock, can produce effects by gradually descending. Again, an elastic body which is stretched or compressed, e.g. a coiled spring or a bent bow, is capable of producing motion by relaxing to its normal state.

Now, from a purely geometrical point of view, a moving body at any instant is indistinguishable from a resting body in the same position at that instant. And, from a purely kinematic point of view, the only difference is the following. Of a moving body we can say, e.g., that at immediately earlier moments it occupied a continuous series of positions to the left of its present position, and that at immediately later moments it will occupy a continuous series of positions to the right of it. Of a resting body we can say that it occupied the same position at immediately earlier moments and will occupy the same position at immediately later moments.

Now it seemed to Leibniz that, if motion is to be real and to have real effects, the state of a moving body at *each instant* must be different from the state of a resting body at an instant. There must be in the moving body, as he puts it, something which is present but which points towards a certain development in the immediate future. The difference at each instant between a moving body and a resting one consists in the presence of *active force* in the former and its absence in the latter. (This is a preliminary rough statement which will have to be made more accurate later.)

Very similar remarks apply to a compressed spring or a raised weight. Although the spring is not doing anything overtly so long as the catch is holding it, it must be in a different internal state from a geometrically similar body which is not compressed but is of its natural length. For it has the power to produce or modify the motions of other bodies whenever it is released. Leibniz gave the name 'active force' to that factor which he thought that we must assume to be present at each moment in a moving body, a compressed spring, or raised weight, and so on, in view of the fact that it is ready to produce effects which would not be produced by a resting body, a relaxed spring, a weight resting on the ground, and so on. I must say that it seems to me plain common sense to regard active force, in this sense, as an essential and independent factor in the notion of corporeal substance.

The following further points about active force should be noted:

(1) Leibniz says that it is not a mere passive potentiality, but an active striving towards a certain process of change in a certain direction. It requires nothing in order to actualize it except the removal of certain hindrances, e.g. the release of a catch, the cutting of a string, etc.

(2) The process of active force in bodies is sometimes obvious to the senses. But reflexion shows that it must be present everywhere in nature even when it is not obvious. Strictly speaking, however, it is something which is never *perceived* by the senses and which cannot be represented by *imagery*. It can only be *conceived* by the intellect on the *occasion* of perceiving certain phenomena with the senses. This seems to me to be true.

(3) Leibniz draws a distinction between what he calls '*primitive* active force' and what he calls '*derived* active force'.[1] I do not want to go into a lot of physical detail, but I think that the essential point is this. He regards each genuine corporeal substance as having a total store of what we should call 'energy', which is neither increased nor diminished by any dynamical transactions in which it may take part. At any moment the whole or part of this will be latent. But at many moments a part of it will be overt. The part which is overt at any moment may take various forms, e.g. it may take the form of the force due to the body moving as a whole (*vis viva*) or the force due to its being compressed or raised, and so on. The proportion of the total energy which is overt at any moment, and the form which that manifestation will then take, depend upon the external conditions in which the body is then placed. The primitive active force is the total store of energy, latent or overt, in the body. The derived active force is the part of this which is overt at any moment. Interaction of body *A* with body *B* merely furnishes the occasion on which so much of *A*'s primitive active force takes such-and-such an overt form, and so much of *B*'s primitive active force takes such-and-such an overt form. There is never any transference of force from one genuine corporeal substance to another.

(4) Leibniz also draws a distinction between what he calls 'living force' (*vis viva*) and 'dead force' (*vis mortua*).[2] There is no doubt at all that what he calls *vis viva* is for all practical purposes what we should nowadays call 'kinetic energy', and not what we should call 'force'. It is measured by the product of the mass of a moving body by the *square* of its velocity. It is not so clear to me what he meant by *vis mortua*, though there is no doubt that he thought that it is illustrated

[1] [G. M., VI, 236. Loemker, 436.]   [2] [G. M., VI, 238. Loemker, 438.]

by systems of bodies which are at rest but in tension or compression, e.g. in a pair of suspended weights connected by a string over a pulley which just balance each other. He says that *vis viva* arises from an infinite series of impressions of *vis mortua*. It is easy to see what he had in mind by taking a simple example. Suppose that a compressed spring lies on a horizontal table with a massive body lying in contact with the free end of it. If the spring is released, it will push the body forward with gradually increasing speed, thus imparting to it more and more *vis viva*. As it does so the tension in it will be gradually relaxed. The *vis mortua* of the spring is certainly *either* the tension itself (which is a force in the modern sense of the word) *or* what we should nowadays call the store of potential energy connected with the tension. It is not clear to me which of the two Leibniz meant by '*vis mortua*'. Probably he did not himself clearly distinguish the two.

(5) Leibniz supports his other arguments for postulating active force in bodies by an argument drawn from the relational theory of space and time. That theory naturally involves a purely relational view of motion. This leads to two arguments at different philosophical levels. They may be stated as follows. (a) Suppose we accept the reality of relations. Let *A* and *B* be two bodies and let the distance between them be increasing at a certain rate. Since distance is a symmetrical relation, this kind of change is perfectly symmetrical as between *A* and *B*. But, if the relational theory be correct, all motion consists simply of changes of distance between bodies. It would therefore appear to be meaningless to say that *A* moved and *B* stood still, or that *A* moved with a certain velocity and *B* moved with a certain other velocity in the same or the opposite direction. Yet common sense would say that a bullet moves and that the target remains at rest. And Newton has empirical arguments for absolute rotation based on the occurrence of centrifugal forces in some cases and their absence in other cases. Leibniz's answer is that this shows that we must postulate something in bodies beside motion. Although motion is nothing but a perfectly symmetrical change of relation between the bodies concerned, the *forces* which are responsible for such changes of relation are something *absolute*. One of the bodies may have all the force which is involved; or each may have some of it in various proportions. That is the real basis of the distinction which is misleadingly described as the difference between 'the absolute true motion' of a body and 'the mere relative change of its situation with respect to another body'.

The kind of thing which Leibniz has in mind is quite obvious. In my example of the bullet and the target the former has the power to break a window or kill a man or set an intervening object in motion, whilst the latter has not. It is the presence of this power in the bullet and its absence in the target which makes us say that the former is absolutely in motion and the latter is not. But, according to Leibniz, when we speak in this way, we are not adding anything intelligible to the fact that the bullet has these dynamical powers and that the target has not.

(b) The second argument would run as follows. Since motion is nothing but change of spatial relations between bodies, and since relations are at best *phenomena bene fundata*, motion itself is at best a *phenomenon bene fundatum*. Therefore there must be in one or other or both of the substances concerned a non-relational attribute whose changes are the foundation of the phenomenon of motion. Leibniz concludes that this must be the active force characteristic of each body.

4.5 Metaphysical implications of Leibniz's dynamics

Leibniz's criticisms on Descartes's doctrine that the essence of corporeal substance is 'extension', i.e. simply geometrical and kinematic properties, seem to me to be annihilating. His criticism of Newton's doctrine of substantival absolute space and time seems to me to be worthy of very serious consideration; and I suppose that, rightly or wrongly, his conclusions on this question would generally be accepted by scientists and philosophers at the present time. Lastly, I am inclined to think that he is right in holding that the notions of what he calls 'passive and active force' are an essential part of what we understand by corporeal substance, and that they cannot be analysed away into anything else. But the question remains whether these facts have the metaphysical implications which Leibniz thinks that they have.

The interpretation which he puts upon them in the *Letters to Arnauld* and other writings of about that period may be summarized as follows.

(1) The notion of *materia prima* in physics is the notion of a continuous, boundless, perfectly homogeneous incompressible fluid, possessing simply the two properties of impenetrability and inertia, i.e. passive force, and the potentiality of movement in the form of circulatory currents within it. This notion is an abstraction from the complete notion of a bodily substance. As we have seen, it is also an essential part of the notion of such a substance to have a store of primitive active forces. This is ready to manifest itself at any moment in this, that, or the other form of derivative active force, according to the external conditions prevailing in the neighbourhood of the body then.

(2) This fits in with the general Scholastic doctrine that a created substance is a composite in which are the two factors of stuff and form. The stuff-factor is those features which constitute *materia prima*, i.e. extension, impenetrability, and inertia. The form-factor, which marks out a particular portion of *materia prima* from the rest as this or that body, is the primitive active force with which it was endowed by God. All its subsequent history consists in the various transformations of this primitive active force, on the occasion of its various encounters with other bodies, and subject to certain general laws which God has impressed on all bodies at their creation.

(3) We must distinguish between a genuine corporeal substance, which is a natural intrinsic unit, and a mere aggregate of several such, which is not. Very often what we take to be a single corporeal substance is an aggregate of many. It might be compared to a flock, whilst a genuine bodily substance may be compared to a single sheep. The primitive active force in a genuine bodily substance is of the nature of a *soul*, and the substance as a whole is of the nature of a *living creature*. The organism of such a living creature, taken apart from its soul, is not a single bodily substance but is an aggregate of many such. But it is an aggregate of a very peculiar kind, which Leibniz calls a 'natural machine'. One peculiarity of a natural machine is that, unlike an artificial one, it can never be generated or altogether destroyed in the course of nature. It can only get larger or smaller, and there is always present in it a certain degree of vitality. Leibniz says explicitly that this is true even of organisms which would not commonly be counted as the bodies of animals.

Thus every natural unit of corporeal substance is an animated natural machine. It resembles the traditional atom in being ingenerable and indestructible. But the traditional atom was conceived either (a) as unextended and punctiform, having no properties except position, motion, mass, and force, or (b) as a homogeneous, continuous, indivisible little body, separated in space from other similar little bodies except on the occasions when they happened to hit each other. According to Leibniz, a natural unit of corporeal substance differs from the traditional atom in having an extended organism differentiated into various parts which are its organs. It differs also in being animated by something of the nature of a soul. This is indivisible, not because it is punctiform but because it is non-spatial and has that kind of internal unity which is characteristic of a mental substance.

What we ordinarily take to be a single bodily substance, e.g. a stone, is of course *not* one of these natural units. It is generally an aggregate of a large number of them, and is not a natural machine and is not animated by a substantial form. It may be compared to a swarm of fish. Only we must remember that what corresponds to the water between the fish, in this analogy, is also an aggregate of natural units. And the medium between them is in turn an aggregate of natural units. And so on without end; for there are no empty spaces. Also we must remember that a natural unit need not be something very small. A human being, e.g., is a natural unit. It is not a question of size but of organization. The question is: 'Is it a natural machine, animated by a substantial form which stands to the machine in an analogous relation to that in which a man's soul stands to his body?'

(4) Although we must postulate a substantial form, analogous to the soul, as an essential factor in every natural unit of corporeal substance, we must not appeal to those substantial forms in explaining any particular natural phenomenon. This was the mistake which the Scholastics made, and from which Galileo and Descartes delivered us. Each particular phenomenon must be explained *mechanically*, i.e. from the general laws of motion and the particular shapes, sizes, masses, spatial relations, and *derived* active forces of the bodies concerned. The shapes, sizes, and masses are determinate modifications of the *stuff*-factor or primitive passive force in bodies. The derivative active forces are determinate modifications of the factor of *substantial form*, i.e. of the primitive active force in bodies. This provides Leibniz with an additional argument for postulating primitive active force. The determinate force which a body (e.g. a compressed spring) exerts on a particular occasion must be an occurrent modification of some persistent determinable property in it, just as its determinate shape or size on any occasion is an occurrent modification of a certain persistent determinable property of it, viz. its extension. But an *active* occurrent cannot be a modification of a merely *passive* persistent determinable. Therefore we must postulate a primitive active force, as the persistent determinable of which the determinate active forces which a body manifests on various occasions are the occurrent modifications.

(5) The laws of motion, which are the universal premisses or principles in the mechanical explanation of particular phenomena, are themselves of *metaphysical* origin. They cannot be derived from merely geometrical or arithmetical considerations. Leibniz gives as examples the principles that 'there is neither more nor less power in the effect than in the cause'; that every change takes place gradually; and that every action is accompanied by an equal and opposite reaction. He calls these 'systematic rules of motion'. I am not sure what he means

by this. Perhaps he means that the actual laws, which state, e.g., that *vis viva* and momentum are conserved, are not *deducible from* these very general principles; but that no law could be true unless it were compatible with them and were in fact a determinate specification of them. He is no doubt right in saying that these 'systematic rules' do not follow from the notions of extension, impenetrability, and inertia. He concludes, rashly I think, that they must follow from the notion of primitive active force, which is the other factor in the complete notion of a bodily substance.

(6) In general we ought not to appeal to final causes, i.e. to the supposed intentions of God, in physics. But Leibniz thinks that there are cases in which it is useful to do so. It is plain from his examples that he is thinking of the principle in optics that light always travels from one point to another by the path which takes the least time to traverse of all the alternative paths open to it, no matter how often it may be reflected or refracted on the way. He says, truly, that by appealing to minimal principles, such as this, we can often reach correct results which it would be difficult to prove by detailed mechanical theories as to what is happening at each intermediate place to date. He evidently regards such principles as characteristic of the wisdom of God, who ordains that an effect shall be produced with the minimum expenditure of time or of some other commodity which men deem valuable.

As regards these alleged metaphysical implications of Leibniz's dynamics I would make the following comments.

(1) If the argument is not to be circular, we must be sure that the dynamical principles, which are supposed to be the basis of it, were reached without tacitly assuming the metaphysical conclusions. I think that this is true in the main. The place where I feel doubtful about it is where Leibniz professes to show that in dynamical transactions between A and B each moves entirely by its own primitive active force, and that the only function of B is to furnish the occasion for so much of the primitive active force of A to manifest itself in such-and-such a determinate overt form. The physical arguments seem to me very thin indeed, and I suspect that the real ground is the metaphysical principle of the impossibility of transeunt causation.

(2) It is admitted that most of the bodies which we can observe in physical experiments are not individual corporeal substances, on Leibniz's view, but are aggregates of vast numbers of them. Therefore the laws of mechanics, as discovered by observation and applied in

practice, must be the laws of *aggregates* of corporeal substances. This fact seems to me to have the two following implications:

(a) It makes one doubt whether it can be safe to base metaphysical theories about the nature of individual corporeal substances on the laws and concepts of empirical dynamics.

(b) It makes one doubt whether Leibniz's dynamical theories are supposed to be true of what we ordinarily take to be bodily substances, e.g. stones, billiard-balls, etc. Are they not perhaps ideal principles which would apply only to the dynamical transactions of genuine individual substances if we were lucky enough to have to do with them?

In general I do not think it could possibly be admitted that the analysis of dynamical facts which Leibniz has made in criticizing Descartes and Newton would suffice by itself to *necessitate* his metaphysical theory of corporeal substances as animated natural machines. I doubt whether it suffices by itself even to suggest or support that theory very strongly. But, of course, Leibniz had other and possibly better reasons. It might be claimed that, whilst none of them separately is conclusive, the dynamical arguments play their part in conjunction with the others in a single interlocking argument which, taken as a whole, is very strong.

5 Endless divisibility

I think that the best statement of Leibniz's argument for substantial forms from the endless divisibility of corporeal substance is in his *Letters to Arnauld* and particularly in his Fifth Letter.[1] By this time Arnauld had raised a number of objections and a certain amount of mutual misunderstanding had been cleared up.

5.1 The argument for intrinsic units

Leibniz says that he takes it as a fundamental principle that every aggregate must in the end be composed of entities each of which is a genuine intrinsic unit. The reason which he gives is this. An aggregate, e.g. a flock of sheep, derives any reality which it has from the elements of which it is composed. For the essence of an aggregate is to be a 'mode of being' of the individuals of which it is composed. And, Leibniz says, anything whose nature is to be a mode of being of something else presupposes the existence of entities whose nature is *not* to

[1] [G. II, 111–27. Loemker, 338–48.]

be a mode of being of something else. I take this to mean: (1) That every intelligible statement in which the name or description of an aggregate occurs could be replaced by a set of statements, with appropriately modified predicates, in which that name or description is absent, but in which names or descriptions of its constituents occur. (2) That in any such analysis it must be possible eventually to come to statements which do not involve either explicit or disguised collective names or descriptions, but only names or descriptions of individuals. Thus, you might at first analyse statements about an army into statements about its regiments, and statements about each regiment into statements about its battalions; and so on. But eventually it must be possible to have an analysis wholly in terms of statements about individual soldiers; and there the process will stop.

Leibniz says that the same principle can be stated in other ways. One is to say that what is not literally *one* entity is not strictly *an* entity at all. Another is to say that the plural presupposes the singular, i.e. that, when there is no entity which naturally counts as *one* so-and-so, there can be no talk of there being *several* so-and-so's.

Arnauld had suggested that the point is a merely verbal one and that it simply depends on how you define 'substance'. Suppose you define a 'substance' as an existent which is neither a quality of, nor a relation between, nor a fact about, nor an occurrent in anything, but which has qualities and occurrents, stands in relations, and is a constituent in facts. Then there is no logical objection to a mere aggregate being called a substance. If and only if you make it part of the *definition* of 'substance' that it is to be a natural intrinsic unit, you will have to deny that a mechanical aggregate is a substance.

Leibniz will not admit this. We can leave out the word 'substance', and put the question in the following way: 'Could anything be an aggregate of aggregates of aggregates . . . without end, where at every stage in this hierarchy the unity of each aggregate is something wholly extrinsic, like the unity of two diamonds set side by side in a ring?' This seems to Leibniz to be self-evidently absurd.

Arnauld had raised the question: 'Might it not be part of the essence of a corporeal substance to have no intrinsic unity?' Leibniz answers as follows. If we admit this, then we must admit that it is of the essence of a body to be an extrinsically unified aggregate of parts, each of which is an extrinsically unified aggregate of parts, and so on without end. In that case the right conclusion would be that there could be nothing answering to the description of a corporeal substance. For this description is not the description of a possible existent. We should therefore have to say that there are no bodies, and that what we take to be bodies are phenomena which are not even *bene fundata*. The status of the ostensibly physical world would be that of a coherent dream. It would not even have that degree of reality which science ascribes to a rainbow. For science would say that, although what we perceive as a rainbow is not a continuous coloured solid arch, as it seems to be, yet it is an aggregate of what science regards as genuine substances, viz. drops of water.

Leibniz sums up the situation as follows. At the first move in the analysis of ostensibly corporeal substance we are faced with the following alternatives. Either what we perceive as a body has ultimate constituents which are natural intrinsic units or it has not. If it has not, it cannot really be what we take it to be; it must be something of a different kind which we partly misperceive and misconceive. We could express that alternative by saying that ostensibly corporeal substances are only phenomena, though they may be *phenomena bene fundata*. If, on the other hand, what we perceive as a body does have ultimate constituents which are intrinsic natural units, then there are *prima facie* three alternative possibilities about these ultimate constituents. (1) That they are literally punctiform, having positive and other qualitative characteristics,.but literally no extension and no shape. (This type of theory was worked out in the eighteenth century by Boscovich.) (2) That they are extended, continuous, homogeneous little lumps which are *intrinsically* indivisible. (This was suggested by the Cartesian Cordemoy.) (3) That they are extended and divisible but non-homogeneous, having an intrinsic natural unity such as that of a living animal. This unity is due to each being informed by a substantial form in somewhat the same way as a human organism is animated by a human soul.

5.2 The intrinsic units are of the nature of living organisms

Leibniz explicitly rejected the Cordemoy atom. It is plainly very difficult to see how any homogeneous continuous body, however small, could be intrinsically indivisible. This, however, is not the reason which Leibniz gives for rejecting it. He holds that every substance must at every moment contain traces of all its past and future states, and that it must mirror the whole universe from its own special point of view. And he does not see how a Cordemoy atom could fulfil those two conditions. In the *Letters to Arnauld* he does not explicitly consider the Boscovich theory of punctiform atoms. His later theory of monads might almost be described as a kind of combination of something like this with the doctrine that corporeal substance is a *phenomenon*, but is a *phenomenon bene fundatum*. In the *Letters to Arnauld* he always leaves open the possibility that what we regard as inorganic matter is just a *phenomenon bene fundatum*. But plainly the theory which he prefers is that of animated natural units.

I will now make some comments on this argument of Leibniz's.

(1) Leibniz had not the least objection to *infinity* as such. He did not think that the notion of actual infinity involves any contradiction; and he delighted to point out actual infinities wherever he could, as rebounding to the credit of God's wisdom and power. What he objected to was *indefiniteness*. It seemed to him that anything that can exist in its own right must be a definite unit, having an intrinsic principle of unity within itself, which marks it off from other existents and maintains its identity through change. Plainly the most obvious examples of this on the macroscopic scale are the bodies of men, the higher animals, and the higher plants, i.e. living organisms. Equally plainly a lump of gold or a volume of water, as it appears to ordinary sense-perception and reflexion based on it, does not answer to these conditions. It seems to be a continuous expanse, divisible in principle in any direction into bits of any size and shape. And its shape as a whole seems to depend simply on the external forces that have acted upon it. This is even more obvious with such creations of speculation as the homogeneous continuous boundless fluid of the Cartesians. It is by definition devoid of all natural 'grain', and that seemed to Leibniz to be fatal to its claims to be an actual existent.

It is true that scientists, reflecting on the nature of bodies, have come to the conclusion that what seems to sense-perception to be a homogeneous and continuous lump of gold or volume of water really consists of a vast number of separate small particles. But that only pushes the question back. If each particle of gold is regarded as a little homogeneous continuous lump, it will in principle be divisible in any direction into bits of any size and shape. And so on.

I think we must agree with Leibniz that the only observable bodies which seem to be natural intrinsic units are the living organisms of men and animals and perhaps plants. The only other bodies which might possibly be suggested are crystals. But visible crystals are certainly aggregates of adjoined smaller crystals; and the growth and self-repair of a crystal has some resemblance to the growth and self-repair of a living organism. It is therefore not at all an unreasonable suggestion that the genuine intrinsic units of corporeal substance at every level are of the nature of living organisms, and that what we regard as a continuous lump of inorganic material, e.g. a bit of gold, is a discontinuous aggregate of tiny organisms of the same kind, like a swarm of bees.

(2) In the *Letters to de Volder* Leibniz explains how he reconciles his doctrine of genuine intrinsic extended units with his doctrine that there are no empty holes in the physical world. The gaps within each organism of a given kind and the gaps between two or more organisms of the same kind are occupied with swarms of smaller organisms. The gaps within each of these smaller organisms and between two or more of them are occupied with swarms of still smaller organisms, and so on without end. Matter is not continuous in the sense in which the space of the geometers is said to be so. For that kind of continuity consists in having no definite units, and being *divisible* in innumerable possible ways but not *actually divided* in any. We have just seen that no real thing could have continuity in that sense. Matter is continuous in the sense that it is actually divided into natural intrinsic extended units; that there is no minimal unit; and that the gaps within and between units of any assigned order of magnitude are occupied by other units of a lower order of magnitude. Leibniz illustrates this in an ingenious way by showing how a volume could be completely filled with spheres of various sizes in contact with each other, if the interstices between spheres of one order of magnitude were occupied by spheres of a lower order, and the interstices between these by spheres of a still lower order, and so on without end.

5.3 Organisms and substantial forms

It might be admitted that if corporeal substance is to be a real independent existent it must have genuine units and that these must be of the nature of living organisms. But the question would still remain: 'Does a living animal necessarily consist of a substantial form informing or animating a bodily machine?' Leibniz of course held that it does, and therefore felt entitled to postulate a substantial form in connexion with each genuine unit of corporeal substance.

5.3.1 Leibniz's own view of substantial forms

There is a great deal of discussion on this question in the *Letters to Arnauld*. I think that Leibniz's views at that period may be summarized as follows.

(1) We start with the one case of the union of a substantial form and stuff into a single natural unit which we know from inside, so to speak. This is the human individual, and in that case the substantial form is the soul and the stuff is the body. Here there are three things to consider, viz. (a) a person's body apart from the soul which animates it, (b) a person's soul apart from the body which it animates, and (c) the person or human individual composed of a soul and a body, with the former animating the latter.

(2) There is no doubt that Leibniz denied that a human body apart from the soul which animates it would be a genuine substance. I think there is no doubt that, unlike the Thomists, he held that the soul apart from the body which it animates would be a genuine substance. As regards the human individual, it seems to me that he regards it as a genuine substance in this *Correspondence*. If I am right, then, he uses the word 'substance' here to cover both the human *soul* itself and the human *individual* composed of the soul and the body which it animates.

(3) He seems to assert in this *Correspondence* that a human soul not only *is* a genuine substance and a natural unit, but also that it *confers* genuine substantiality and unity upon the whole composed of itself and the body which it animates, i.e. on the human individual.

(4) In answer to a question by Arnauld, Leibniz explicitly denies that the soul confers genuine unity and substantiality on the *body* which it animates. A human body, alive or dead, is not a genuine substance, though it is composed of genuine substances of a non-human kind.[1] In spite of this denial, I cannot help thinking that Leibniz often talks as if a living organism were a genuine substance which derives its unity and substantiality from the soul which animates it.

(5) If there are any genuine corporeal substances besides human individuals, each of them must be constructed on the same general plan as a human individual. It must consist of something *analogous* to a human soul standing to something *analogous* to a human body in a relation *analogous* to that of animating. We must remember that Leibniz held that the human soul is not concerned merely with the voluntary movements of the limbs, the tongue, etc. It is also concerned in the biological functions of the human body as a living organism, e.g. its conversion of food and air into parts of itself, its self-regulation and self-repair, and so on.

(6) The question arises: 'How far do these analogies go and at what points do they break down?' Leibniz admits and asserts that human

[1] [G., II, 75. Mason, 93.]

souls have many peculiarities. The most important of these are the
process of rational thinking, of self-consciousness, and of personal
memory, with all that these imply. But he thinks that a characteristic
common and peculiar to every substantial form from the highest to
the lowest is the power of representing simultaneously, from its own
particular point of view, a number of other substances, in fact *every*
other substance. In human souls this representative function takes the
form of sense-perception from a particular perspective. But Leibniz
thinks that this is a very special and high grade of it. Now, in the
case of a human individual, the body is the centre from which and
the organ by which the soul perceives everything else from a certain particular point of view. If there are any genuine corporeal
substances in the world beside human individuals, the body of each
must be the centre from which and the organ by which the substantial form represents everything else from a certain particular point
of view.

(7) Leibniz takes the commonsense view, as against the Cartesians,
that non-human animals have souls. If that is granted, it follows at
once that there is a whole range of corporeal substances constructed
on the same general plan as a human individual, i.e. psycho-physical
individuals composed of a soul and an organism which it animates. In
that case there must be a whole descending series of souls, from those
of intelligent apes, which are almost human in many respects, down
to those of oysters and tapeworms. Since there is no clear lower end or
limit to this series, it becomes more or less plausible to conceive the
possibility of its extending further downwards and including, e.g.,
substantial forms of individual cells. Finally, it may extend still further
to include substantial forms of molecules or atoms, which we commonly regard as inorganic.

(8) Leibniz explicitly says that a living human body is not itself a
corporeal substance, but a collection of such.[1] Let us suppose, e.g.,
that it is a collection of living cells. If a cell is a genuine substance, it
too must consist of something analogous to a soul and something
analogous to a body. The body of a single cell in turn will not be a
corporeal substance, but at best a collection of living organisms. Each
of these in turn will have something analogous to a soul and something
analogous to a body. And so on without end.

[1] [G., II, 72. Mason, 88.]

5.3.2 Why postulate a substantial form for each living organism?

Arnauld was not satisfied that it is either necessary or useful to postulate a substantial form in connexion with everything which has the characteristics of a living organism. It must be admitted, he says, that no body has intrinsic unity in the sense in which a soul has it. But there are various degrees of that imperfect kind of unity which is appropriate to bodies. E.g. a watch has a higher degree of such unity than a heap of stones, and the body of a living animal has a higher degree of it than a watch. From the nature of the case such unity must be of the extrinsic mechanical kind. But that is no objection to it. 'The greatest perfection which a body can have is to be a machine so perfect that only God could have made it.' That is the only kind of unity which even a living human body, *as such*, can have. The fact that it is animated by a soul may bestow a *further* unity upon it, but this cannot be of the kind which belongs to the soul itself.

In a certain sense this argument is beside the point. Leibniz admits that there is nothing in the world of corporeal substance except machines, if a 'machine' is defined as an aggregate of spatially inter-related substances, whose characteristic modes of behaviour are de-ducible from the structure, arrangement, and inherent forces of its parts, and the laws of mechanics. He does indeed hold that every natural, as distinct from artificial, machine, must be animated by a substantial form. But he does not hold that the substantial form con-verts the *machine which it animates* into a single substance instead of an aggregate of substances; still less that it gives to it the kind of unity which is characteristic of a soul. What he holds is that the substantial form makes the *whole composed of itself and the machine which it animates* into a single natural psycho-physical unit. In the case of a man, e.g., this unit has the characteristic unity of a *person or individual*, not that of a soul and not that of a machine.

Nevertheless it seems to me that Leibniz's position is very un-satisfactory. I will try to state in my own way the difficulties which I feel. The real question at issue seems to me to be this. Is it necessary or useful to postulate something analogous to a soul in connexion with everything that has the kind of unity which is characteristic of a living organism? Let us grant, for the sake of argument, that it is necessary and useful to postulate a soul, on grounds of introspection in one's own case and on grounds of analogy in the case of other men and the higher animals, in order to deal with the *psychological* facts about them.

Is it necessary or useful to do so in respect of the purely *biological and physiological* facts about them?

The facts are of the following kind. An animal develops from a small speck of material by a regular process, until it reaches the characteristic shape, size, and internal structure of its species. It does this by taking in foreign matter, converting it into flesh, blood, tissues, etc. of various kinds, and building these up with various organs, such as heart, liver, lungs, etc. After this it continues to take in foreign material and convert it into its own substance, replacing in this way wastage; so that in the course of a few years there may be hardly any material in its body that has not been replaced. During the whole of its life it adjusts itself most delicately to changes in the temperature, pressure, etc. of its surroundings, so as to maintain a practically constant internal temperature, salinity of the blood, and so on. If it is injured not too seriously the injured parts heal. After a time the organism performs its self-maintaining and self-repairing functions less and less efficiently and eventually it no longer performs them at all. Then it dies and breaks up.

Now all this looks as if a mind, which desired that there should be an animal of such-and-such a kind, and which had a marvellous knowledge and control of matter, continually directed certain physical processes in such a way as to carry out its plan. It looks as if it were able to succeed for a time, often in face of considerable obstacles; but that sooner or later it always loses grip or interest in the case of each individual of a species. It looks, however, as if it had foreseen and provided for this also by the device of reproduction, whereby each individual produces new individuals of the same kind as itself which will replace it. An artificial machine is always the product of a mind which desires to produce a certain result, and which makes use of its knowledge of the laws and properties of bodies and its power of shaping and arranging them, in order to bring about that result by their interactions. The more you insist on the analogy of a living body to a machine, the more strongly you suggest that there is a mind which stands to it in an analogous relation to that in which a working engineer stands to a machine which he has planned and built and maintained.

So much for the admitted facts; now for philosophical speculation. When a person ascribes a substantial form to a living organism he may be intending one of two things. (1) He may merely be summing up the facts in a compendious form, and saying that the development, self-maintenance, self-repair, and reproduction of living organisms go on in certain respects *as if* these processes were desired and planned and controlled by a mind. Or (2) he may be professing to account for the facts by *actually postulating* such a mind. I suspect that one and the same person may sometimes mean to assert no more than (1) and sometimes as much as (2), and that he may hover between the two without knowing it. We can confine our attention to the second alternative. I shall try to show that it is extremely difficult to accept on any view, and especially so in view of Leibniz's other principles.

(1) Plainly any mind which could do what is required of it by ordinary processes of deliberate planning and construction would need to have a supernatural knowledge of the laws of physics and the details of the physical environment at a given time and place. I suppose that it might be very much limited in its other interests, but in its own small department it would have to be divinely gifted. It seems odd to postulate one such mind for every cat, dog, flea, tapeworm, etc.

(2) How would the mind which looks after the biological processes of an organism be related to the mind which is the subject of its ordinary psychological processes? In one's own case it is perfectly clear that the mind which is open to introspection, and which makes and carries out ordinary plans, does not and could not *consciously* design and carry out the development, maintenance, and repair of one's body. Either we must postulate a different mind, or we must say that the biological functions and the introspectible psychological functions are carried out by different departments of the same mind. Neither alternative is very attractive.

(3) When a man designs and constructs a machine he carries out his plan by making appropriate movements with his fingers, etc., and thus altering in a planned way the mutual relations of foreign bodies. Thus, for a mind to carry out a plan in the ordinary way it must already animate an organism and voluntarily control the movements of certain of its organs. What is the analogy to this in the case of a mind which is supposed to construct and maintain its own organism?

(4) The difficulties may be summed up in the following dilemma. Either you assume that the mind which looks after the biological processes of an organism forms its plans and carries them out as we do when we design and build and maintain a machine, or you assume that it does so in some wholly different way. On the first alternative your hypothesis is intelligible, but, when one considers it in detail, it proves to be quite incredible. On the second alternative it is not intelligible if it is intended as an explanation of the admitted facts. At

best it is merely a summary of those facts masquerading as a hypothesis to explain them.

(5) It seems to me that all these difficulties would exist for Leibniz, but that there would also be the following additional difficulty. There is no point in postulating a kind of soul to look after the biological processes of each living organism unless it can directly or indirectly influence the body and foreign bodies which it absorbs. But on Leibniz's general principles it cannot possibly do this. If everything in a living organism would go on exactly as it does even if it were not animated by a soul, what evidence can there be for postulating a soul in connexion with every living organism? It is no answer to say that each of us has introspective evidence for a soul in his own case, and that it is reasonable to argue by analogy to the presence of a soul in every kind of living organism. The soul for which each of us has introspective evidence is known as something which is responsible for one's *mental* life and for one's rational speech and deliberate action. It is not known as something which is responsible for the growth, main- tenance, self-repair, and reproduction of one's body.

It seems to me that we may divide Leibniz's argument here into the following steps. (1) Corporeal substance must be composed of bodies each of which is a natural intrinsic unit. (2) Any such unit must be of the nature of a living creature. (3) The body of a living creature is an aggregate which is a natural machine; and the characteristic unity of a living creature arises from the fact that there is something analogous to a soul standing to this natural machine in a relation analogous to that in which a human soul stands to its body. The first and the second steps seem to me to be plausible. But the third is logically independent of it, and I do not find it at all plausible. It seems to me that there is ground for postulating something analogous to a soul where and only where there is ground for assuming some kind of consciousness in connexion with the processes in and the behaviour of a living creature. I cannot see that Leibniz has shown that there need be any kind of consciousness in connexion with organisms and organic processes as such, and therefore I cannot see any reason to postulate something analogous to a soul in the case of everything which has the character- istics of a living creature.

6 Argument for substantial forms from the Predicate-in-Notion Principle

Leibniz asserts that the Predicate-in-Notion Principle requires us to postulate a substantial form in any genuine substance. I do not find the argument very clearly stated anywhere, but I think that it must be of the following kind.

I said, when discussing the Principle, that I think that Leibniz puts the following interpretation on it. He thinks of every substance as being created with a stock of innate dispositions which are, so to speak, the ontological correlate of the various facts in its complete notion. Now we are familiar enough with the notion of a *soul* carrying traces of past experiences which emerge from time to time as conscious memory-experiences. It is extremely difficult to see how such disposition could be carried by the single homogeneous continuous fluid of Descartes, or the many little continuous homogeneous separate atoms of Cordemoy, or indeed by any purely corporeal substance. I suspect therefore that Leibniz held that we must postulate something like a mind or soul in connexion with every genuine substance for the following reason. It is needed in order to retain, by something analogous to memory, the initial dispositions which God gave to it at its creation. These dispositions at the appropriate dates in its subsequent history give rise spontaneously to the states which it is part of its complete notion to have at those dates. This may be compared to traces of past experiences giving rise to actual memory-experiences when a suitable cue is provided, e.g. by the occurrence of an associated idea.

7 Substantial forms and organic bodies are ingenerable and incorruptible

Leibniz held that every substantial form is naturally ingenerable and incorruptible. It can come into existence only through a creative act of God and can cease to exist only if God decides to annihilate it by a miracle. The reason which he generally gives is that it is not extended and therefore cannot come into existence by the coming together of previously separated components and cannot cease to exist by the separation of its component parts. It is indeed obvious that nothing like a mind or soul could come into existence by composition or cease to exist by decomposition. But it is not clear that these are the only conceivable natural ways of beginning or ceasing to exist.

This argument was accepted by almost all Leibniz's contemporaries as regards the human soul, and he simply applied it, quite consistently, to all substantial forms. He claims also that the same proposition follows from the Predicate-in-Notion Principle. I cannot see that it follows that a substance could not cease to exist in the course of nature. Why should it not be part of the notion of a substance, implanted in it at its creation, that it should cease to exist at a certain moment when other substances in its neighbourhood had reached a certain stage in their own internal development?

Now Leibniz held not only that every living organism must be animated by a kind of soul but also that every kind of soul must at every moment of its existence animate a living organism. I cannot see that he has any satisfactory argument for the latter proposition. I think that one cause of his belief may be the following confusion. According to the Scholastics, the notions of form and stuff are correlative factors in the notion of substance. Even in the case of a human being it is the *person*, as a psycho-physical individual, which is a substance. The soul, which is the substantial form of the body, is not by itself a substance. On that kind of view it is readily intelligible that every soul requires an organism; the surprising thing is that a human soul should be able to exist, even temporarily and abnormally, without an organism, between the death of a man and the resurrection of his body at the Last Judgment. But Leibniz, though keeping the names of 'substantial form' and 'stuff', has made substantial forms into complete substances. It is not clear why a soul, if it is a complete substance and not merely a correlative factor to the stuff-factor in a substance, should need always to animate a body.

I suspect that Leibniz's main reason for this doctrine might be stated as follows. It is of the essence of a soul to represent the rest of the world from a particular point of view. But a soul without a body would have no particular point of view; for it only occupies a particular position in the world indirectly through animating a body which occupies a particular position. I think that this argument might be plausible on the ordinary view that the soul acts on the external world only by acting on its body, and perceives the external world only through being acted upon by its body. But it is a good deal less plausible when combined with Leibniz's view that the soul neither affects nor is affected by the body.

7.1 Theory of Transformation of Bodies

The combination of the three propositions that every substantial form is ingenerable and indestructible, that every natural unit of corporeal substance has its own substantial form, and that no substantial form ever exists without animating a living body led Leibniz to his curious theory of *Transformation*.

Arnauld raised a great number of difficulties, of which the following are typical. What happens to the substantial form of a worm when the worm is cut in two and each half becomes a living worm? Do the souls of innumerable flies, gnats, lice, etc. continue to exist indefinitely after the death of their bodies? Do animal souls exist, indivisible and indestructible in the semen of every animal? If so, what happens to them (a) in cases where semen is emitted without leading to conception, or (b) in the case of a male animal who dies without ever having sexual intercourse with a female? What happens to the substantial form of a creature when its body is burnt to ashes, which are purely inorganic material, e.g. the ram which Abraham sacrificed as a burnt-offering in place of Isaac?

Leibniz's theory, in answer to all such questions, is as follows. He draws a distinction between his own theory of *Transformation of Bodies* and the old Pythagorean theory of *Transmigration of Souls*. The Pythagorean theory is that, at the death of a man or animal, the soul which had animated its body leaves the corpse altogether, joins up with an embryo (of the same or another species) which has just been conceived, and begins to animate it. Leibniz naturally disapproved of this theory as involving serious breaches of the Principle of Continuity as applied to changes. His own alternative is the following.

The soul of any living creature which will ever exist in the course of history was created once for all at the beginning of the world, and will persist (barring miracles) until the end of the world. At every moment it animates a living body of *some* kind. When a living creature A dies its soul continues to animate a very small part of its former body. The result is a microscopic or ultra–microscopic living creature α, which need bear no more resemblance to A than a tadpole does to a frog. After such a reduction in scale the creature lives a very restricted life and its perception and activities are very limited. In the same way, what we call the generation of a new living creature B is really a rapid transformation and growth of a microscopic or ultra-microscopic creature β which already existed and was animated by the same soul.

We can occasionally observe transformations of this kind on the macroscopic scale, e.g. when a tadpole becomes a frog or a maggot becomes a moth. If one could see by means of an ultra-microscope the little animal to which Abraham's ram was reduced when its body was burned, there is no reason why it should look like a little ram. It might look no more like a ram than a maggot looks like a moth. Since the microscope reveals swarms of minute living organisms in every drop of apparently pure water, we need have no difficulty in finding room at every moment for all the transformed macroscopic animals which have lived and died since the creation.

It is an empirical question whether the ultra-microscopic residual organism which is animated by the soul of a dead macroscopic animal will ever develop into another macroscopic animal. If it should do so, it is another empirical question whether it will develop into a macroscopic animal of the same kind as the one which died and with which it was continuous. Leibniz does not profess to be able to answer these questions, but the fact that he cannot do so is no objection to his general theory.

Leibniz does not maintain that there is any one portion of corporeal substance which is constantly attached to a given substantial form. The stuff in the organism of any soul is continually changing, rather slowly at normal times, and very quickly at certain critical periods; and there is no reason to suppose that any part of it remains there for ever. In the *Letters to des Bosses* Leibniz says definitely that the phrase 'same body' must be understood in the sense of 'same river', when we say that a given substantial form perpetually animates the same body.[1]

The body of any living creature, great or small, is an aggregate and not a substance. It must be composed of genuine intrinsic units. Each such unit must be of the nature of an animal with a soul and a body. Therefore the body of any living creature, e.g. a cat, is an aggregate of other living creatures. These are not little cats, but are other kinds of living creatures for which we have no names. But the soul which animates a body, which is an aggregate of living creatures, is not itself composed of the souls of those living creatures.

A corpse is what remains of a body, formerly animated by a certain soul, when that soul has ceased to animate the whole aggregate and now animates only an ultra-microscopic part of it. So a corpse is neither a genuine substance, nor is it the stuff-factor in a genuine substance, as a living body is. It is a *mere* aggregate. But it is not merely a delusive appearance; for it is composed of genuine substances, each of which has intrinsic unity because it is a living body animated by a substantial form.

As regards an animal which is burned to ashes, Leibniz says that there is no reason why ashes, or any other composite mass of material which is inorganic as a whole, should not contain or even entirely consist of living creatures. Indeed, if Leibniz's general theory is true, it must do so unless it is a mere *phenomenon*.

As regards the worm which is cut in two, Leibniz answers cautiously

[1] [G., II, 370. Loemker, 597.]

as follows. We need not assume that both halves are alive because both continue to squirm about for a while. The soul will certainly not be divided into two, and, if it animates either half, it will certainly not animate more than one of the two.

As regards animals which are certainly reproduced sexually Leibniz makes the following remarks. The microscopists Leeuwenhoek and Swammerdam (who first observed spermatozoa at about the time of Leibniz's correspondence with Arnauld) are inclined to think that a macroscopic animal arises through the transformation of a microscopic animal, viz. a spermatozoon of the male parent. (It should be remembered that spermatozoa were observed long before ova were observed and identified. It was thought that the function of the female in reproduction was only to provide the receptacle in which the spermatozoon undergoes its transformation, and the stimuli and nutriment needed for these transformations.) So far then Leibniz's theory seemed to have the support of the best embryologists of his time. It is indeed plain that Leibniz was much impressed and influenced by the revelations which the microscope was making at this period.

Leibniz admits that the microscopists have never given explicit support to his correlative view, viz. that the *death* of a macroscopic animal is a process of transformation to a microscopic one animated by the same soul. His explanation is as follows. The lack of empirical support is not surprising. The process of involution at death is much less easy to observe than the process of evolution during gestation. The former takes place suddenly and quickly, whilst the latter does so gradually.

The last point to be noticed is that Leibniz thinks that spirits, i.e. rational souls, such as those of men and angels, are in many respects peculiar. In the *Letters to Arnauld* he suggests that God creates spirits when he thinks fit in the course of the history of the world.[1] I take it that this would be at the conception of each human embryo. He also says that at the death of a man God detaches the spirit from the body 'or at any rate from the *gross* body'.[2] This was not his final view, and we will defer his account of rational souls till later.

[1] [G., II, 100. Mason, 125.]   [2] [ibid.]

4
THEORY OF MONADS

The theory of corporeal substance which I have been describing comes mainly from the *Discours de métaphysique* (1685) and the *Correspondence with Arnauld* (1686–90), supplemented by Leibniz's writings on dynamics and the *Correspondence with Clarke* for the special points which are treated there. In its main outline he continued to hold this theory; but there were important changes of detail and to some extent of principle in his later works.

I think that Leibniz's doctrine at this stage might be described as primarily *panorganic* and secondarily *animistic*. It seems to me that Leibniz held that there really are corporeal substances, but that every such substance is a *living organism*. That is why I call the theory 'primarily panorganic'. It is 'secondarily animistic' because he held that each living organism must have its own substantial form, and that a substantial form is a substance of the nature of a soul. Even at this stage Leibniz held that most of the objects which we take to be corporeal substances are not really so, and he frequently mentions as a possible view that everything which we take to be an inorganic body is only a *phenomenon bene fundatum* comparable to a rainbow. But he never asserts that theory, and I think his general position is that what we take to be an inorganic body consists of a collection of substances each of which *really is* corporeal, though it is *something more* because it is animated by a kind of soul.

It seems to me that the later development was from a theory which is panorganic and animistic to a theory which is still panorganic and animistic but is *panpsychic*. The only genuine substances are now of the nature of souls and there are really no corporeal substances. Certain aggregates of souls appear to certain other souls as extended massive movable substances. What we take to be bodies, whether organic or inorganic, are at best *phenomena bene fundata*. This theory is stated in terms of 'monads', a word which, so far as I can discover, does not occur in the *Discours* or the *Letters to Arnauld*. This word begins to occur in the *Letters to John Bernoulli* (1698–9), and it is regularly used in the *Letters to de Volder* (1699–1706).

The Theory of Monads is one of the most elaborate and all-embracing systems of constructive metaphysics that exist, and the brief statement of it in the *Monadology* (about 1712) is a triumph of condensed exposition. But it is much easier to appreciate it when one sees it in relation to the earlier theories out of which it developed.

1 Monads and entelechies

So far as I know the first place in which the word 'monad' occurs is in the *Correspondence with John Bernoulli*.[1] A monad is there defined as 'a substance which is truly one, i.e. not an aggregate of substances'.[2] I do not think that the *definition* is ever altered. Thus in the *Letters to de Volder* a monad is described as 'a complete simple substance';[3] in the *Letters to des Bosses* it is described as 'a perfect substance';[4] and in the *Monadology* as 'a simple substance, i.e. one without parts'.[5] This undoubtedly means something which *is* a substance and is not composed of *other substances*.

But I think that there is a profound change in Leibniz's views of the nature of the entities which answer to this definition. In the *Letters to Bernoulli* Leibniz says: 'I call a monad . . . not so much the soul as the animal itself or something analogous, provided with a soul and an organic body.'[6] He adds that every animal is a substance, and that neither a man nor a dog is composed of the parts of its body. This seems to be the doctrine which we have already described in the *Discours* and the *Letters to Arnauld*. The name 'monad' seems here simply to be used of any living creature consisting of a soul animating an organic body. But this is quite certainly not Leibniz's later view.

The change occurs in the *Letters to de Volder*. These extend over the seven years from 1699 to 1706. I do not feel sure that the doctrine of the later years is consistent with that of the earlier ones; but I think that there is no doubt that, as the correspondence goes on, Leibniz explicitly reaches a quite different view which he retained thereafter. It involves a new technical term, viz. *entelechy*. This is taken from Aristotle, and Leibniz has often used it before, but he now makes the meaning more definite. Unfortunately, as it seems to me, he does not use it consistently. When he is being careful he distinguishes 'entelechy'

---

1 [This is not quite correct. Cf. Loemker, 508 n11.]
2 [G. M., III, 537.]   3 [G., II, 252. Loemker, 530.]
4 [G., II, 306.]   5[G., II, 607. Loemker, 643.]
6 [G. M., III, 542.]

from 'monad', and regards an entelechy as an inseparable factor in a monad. But it seems to me that he often uses it carelessly as equivalent to 'monad'.

In a very important passage in the *Letters to de Volder* Leibniz distinguishes the following four kinds of entity in connexion with any living being.[1] (1) A primitive entelechy or soul. (2) The *materia prima*, or primitive passive force, which is the stuff of which the entelechy is the form. (3) The dominant monad, which is composed of these two factors. (4) The organic machine, which is an aggregate of innumerable monads, each composed of an entelechy and *materia prima*. The dominant monad stands to the monads in the organic machine in a peculiar relation which he expresses by saying that it is *dominant* in respect of them and they are *subordinate* in respect of it. The living being or animal consists of the dominant monad together with the subordinate monads which together constitute the organic machine. Leibniz here describes it as 'the corporeal substance which is made one by the dominant monad in the organic machine'. It is evident then that we have two entirely different relationships. One holds *within* each monad between the entelechy and the *materia prima*. Neither of these is a substance, but they are two inseparable factors in a substance related as form to stuff. The other relation holds between a certain monad and all the other monads in a certain aggregate. This is the relation within a living being between one monad, which is dominant, and the rest which are subordinate to it. Although the doctrine of the *Letters to des Bosses* differs in important points of detail, it agrees completely about the internal structure of the monad. Leibniz says there that each entelechy has its own *materia prima*; that together they constitute a monad; and that, whilst God could deprive a dominant monad of its subordinate monads, he could not deprive an entelechy of its *materia prima* or create an entelechy without *materia prima*.[2]

It is now easy to understand why Leibniz, when he is not being specially careful, is liable to talk of 'entelechies' when he means 'monads'. He has said that an entelechy is of the nature of a soul, and this must be taken along with the Aristotelian and Scholastic doctrine that the relation of a soul to the body which it animates is that of a substantial form to the stuff which it informs. In the light of this we might say that an entelechy is the soul of an individual monad, whilst a dominant monad is the soul of the individual composed of itself and the subordinate monads which constitute its organism. But the phrase 'is the soul of' has different implications in these two statements. When

---

[1] [G., II, 252. Loemker, 530–1.]   [2] [G., II, 324–5.]

we say that an entelechy is the soul of an individual monad, we are speaking in terms of the Aristotelian theory that soul and body are not two substances but are the form-factor and the stuff-factor in a single substance. When we say that a dominant monad is the soul of a man or a cat or any other living creature we are speaking in terms of the Platonic and Cartesian theory that a soul is a substance and that the body which it animates is another substance or collection of substances. In the end Leibniz has accepted both views, one for the internal structure of the individual monad, and the other for the relation of soul and body in a living creature.

2 Corporeal substance is a phenomenon bene fundatum

The next important change to be noted is that Leibniz definitely comes to the conclusion that corporeal substance is only a *phenomenon bene fundatum*. In the earlier works this view has constantly been in the offing as a possible alternative. But the line taken there was that corporeal substance would be something more than a *phenomenon bene fundatum* if and only if it was admitted that every genuine corporeal substance is an animated organism. He assumed that such an organism really would have the properties which scientists ascribe to bodies, viz. shape, size, position, motion, impenetrability, inertia, and various kinds of potential energy, though it would not have the secondary qualities of colour, temperature, etc. His new position may be stated as follows. He gives up nothing that he had asserted about the necessity of having natural intrinsic units, and about such units being animated organisms. But he now holds that even an organism cannot really have even those properties which scientists ascribe to bodies. Suppose that I am in a situation in which it would be true to say of me in ordinary speech that I am seeing and touching a cat, and where there is no question of my being asleep and dreaming or delirious or subject to an optical delusion, etc. Leibniz would now say: You certainly are perceiving a collection of substances which exist independently of you. Those substances certainly do have, independently of you, certain properties which are correlated respectively with the shape, size, position, motion, etc. which you ostensibly perceive. But neither separately nor collectively do they have shape, size, position, motion, etc. They do *not* have the properties which you perceive them as having, or which a physicist would ascribe to them on the basis of those which you perceive them as having. And they *do* have other properties, viz. mental ones, which you do not perceive them as having and which they seem to you *not* to have. This is what he means by saying that bodies are only *phenomena*, though they are *phenomena bene fundata*. A more accurate way of stating the case would be this. There are no bodies. But there are independent substances or collections of substances which human beings misperceive as bodies. And, when a person's perceptions answer to the ordinary tests for normality, the various properties which *appear to him* to belong to the object which he *misperceives* as a body are correlated with certain properties which *really do* belong to that object.

This view and the main argument for it are stated very clearly in the *Letters to de Volder*. Anything that can be subdivided is an aggregate composed of several constituents. Anything that is an aggregate lacks intrinsic unity; it has unity only for the mind of an observer and relatively to his special interests and perceptual limitations. The reality of an aggregate is entirely borrowed from that of its constituents. Therefore anything that can be subdivided has no reality unless it has constituents which do not consist of a plurality of coexisting parts.[1] I will complete the argument as follows.

Consider any ostensible body, whether organic or inorganic. It is part of the notion of a body to be extended. Either this ostensible body is continuous or it is discrete. If it is discrete, it will consist of a number of scattered smaller bodies, each of which is extended and continuous; and we can apply the argument that follows to them. So we can confine our attention to ostensible bodies which are continuous. Now any volume, however small, consists of smaller volumes which together exactly make it up without overlapping. Therefore, if any volume, however small, be completely filled with corporeal substance, the substances which fill it must be an aggregate composed of the smaller bits of corporeal substance which respectively fill the smaller volumes which together make up this volume without overlapping. But, for precisely the same reason, each of these smaller bits of corporeal substance would in turn be an aggregate of smaller bits, and so on without end. Therefore a continuous extended substance would be an aggregate of aggregates of aggregates . . . without end. This is an impossible condition and therefore there cannot be any extended substances. Therefore, whenever we perceive or conceive anything as extended we must be to that extent *mis*perceiving it or *mis*conceiving it.

This argument seems to me to be important for the following reasons. (1) It is a purely *ontological* argument against the reality of corporeal substance, and not a merely epistemological argument like Berkeley's. (2) It is quite independent of whether the ostensibly

[1] [G., II, 267. Cf. also 261.]

extended objects are animated organisms or not. Let them be as animated and as organic as they will, if their organisms are held to be extended, they are open to this objection. (3) If valid, it would be fatal to Cordemoy's extended homogeneous little atoms. The fact that it is *physically* impossible to *separate* the parts of a Cordemoy atom is irrelevant to the argument.

Leibniz draws precisely the right conclusion from his argument. He says that we must postulate unextended entities as *constitutive* of ostensible bodies. But we must not say that bodies are *composed of* these constitutive entities. It would obviously be self-contradictory to say that an extended object was *composed of* unextended parts; for the whole point of the argument is that, *if* an object were extended, then, however small it might be, it would consist of parts which are also *extended*. What we must say is that certain aggregates of these unextended substances present to us the delusive appearance of being extended, movable, massive substances, i.e. bodies. The monads are not *parts* of bodies; for there can be no such things as bodies for them to be parts of, and, if there could be, they could not have unextended parts. The monads are the real foundations of the partly delusive experiences in which we seem to ourselves to perceive bodies.

3 Plurality of substances

Why did Leibniz hold that there is a plurality of substances instead of holding, like Spinoza, that there is only one genuine substance? He was, of course, quite familiar with Spinoza's doctrine and he occasionally refers to it in his correspondence. Thus, e.g., de Volder at one stage threw out the suggestion that perhaps only the whole universe is a substance. To this Leibniz answered[1] (1) that this is contrary to the usual meaning of the word 'substance'; (2) that 'B. de S.' has produced no shadow of reason for this doctrine; and (3) that, if anyone wants to use 'substance' in this odd way, we can let him do so and say that there are a number of 'things' or 'subjects' in each of which there are 'modes' (i.e. occurrents).

I believe that Leibniz's main reasons for Pluralism were the following.

(1) He understood by the term 'substance' a continuant which *has* occurrents or states (i.e. what he would call 'modes'), but *is* not itself an occurrent in or a state of anything. Now it seemed to him obvious that his own mind was a continuant, having various experiences as

[1] [G., II, 257–8. Loemker, 532.]

occurrents in it. And he did not doubt that there are other finite minds besides his own. In the *Letters to des Bosses* he says that he can judge that he is not the only created existent because he can see that there is no reason why he should be in the privileged position of being the only substance actually created.[1] Now it seemed to him meaningless to suggest, as Spinoza had in effect done, that all finite minds are occurrents in a single Mental Continuant. If you suppose that this single Mental Continuant is a *mind* and that our minds are *experiences* in it, the suggestion is plainly nonsensical. If you say, as Spinoza did, that it is mental but is not a mind, it is doubtful whether you have any clear idea of what you are asserting. So I take it that Leibniz took a pluralistic view about ordinary minds, at any rate, on plain common-sense grounds.

(2) Passing to ostensibly material objects, we have to account for the fact that they *appear* to be extended and endlessly divisible into co-existing parts. Granted that nothing can really have this property, we have to account for the appearances. It is reasonable to do this in such a way as to reduce the degree of misperception to a minimum. Now Leibniz has no objection to *infinity* as such. What he objects to is a compound whose components are themselves compounds, and so on without end. His solution is to suppose that any ostensibly extended substance, no matter how small it may appear to be when it is mis-perceived as extended, is in fact an aggregate of an infinite number of simple unextended substances. His suggestion is that the harmless infinity of an infinite aggregate of simple unextended substances is misperceived by us as something which would have the objectionable infinity of a compound composed of compounds which are themselves compounds without end. If we accept this argument Leibniz has given good reason for thinking that there is an infinite number of substances, each of which is simple in the sense that it does not consist of coexisting parts and therefore is not extended.

4 Characteristics of monads

So far as the argument has gone the simple substances at the basis of the appearance of extended objects might be spatially punctiform entities; having spatial position, mobility, inertia, and various inherent active forces, but no spatial extension. A physical theory on those lines was worked out in detail by Boscovich[2] and in less detail by Kant in his

---

[1] [G., II, 516.]

[2] [*Theoria Philosophiae Naturalis* (Venice, 1763).]

Metaphysical Bases of Natural Science. But it was not Leibniz's view. He held that the simple substances are *minds or souls.* We must now consider this part of his doctrine.

4.1 Monads are minds

The following is a very clear statement of Leibniz's doctrine, taken from the *Letters to de Volder.* He says that the simple substances which are the foundation of the phenomena of matter and motion do not differ essentially from our own souls, which we know from within. There is nothing in the ostensibly external world except simple substances, and nothing in any simple substances except *appetition* and *perception.*[1] We must now consider why Leibniz ascribes these two properties to every monad, and what precisely he means by doing so.

4.1.1 Appetition

Leibniz holds that it is of the essence of a created substance to be continually in process of change of state. There is a strong statement of this view in the *Letters to de Volder.* 'Nothing else in a finite substance is permanent, on my view, except that law itself which involves continual sequence. . . .'[2] Now changes must be caused, and there can be no transeunt causation. Therefore each total state of a monad must be completely determined by its immediate predecessor and must completely determine its immediate successor. The law or pattern of all its future changes was impressed on the monad by God at its creation. But that would not suffice. He must have endowed it with a permanent active tendency to pass from one total state to another in accordance with the innate law or pattern. Leibniz calls this active tendency, which keeps up the series of purely immanent changes, *Appetition.* It might be compared to what Spinoza called *Conatus.* We must not think of it as a deliberate striving to bring about an imagined and desired future state of oneself. That is a very special form of appetition which can occur only in the higher kinds of monad which are capable of memory and imagination.

4.1.2 Perception

Leibniz explains in Section 14 of the *Monadology* that he is using the word 'perception' in a very extended and technical sense when he

[1] [G., II, 270. Loemker, 537.]   [2] [G., II, 263. Loemker, 534.]

ascribes perception to every simple substance.[1] Perception, as it occurs in human beings in normal attentive working life, is a very special form of it. He says that the essential peculiarity of perception is that 'multiplicity is represented in unity'. This notion of representation of multiplicity in unity goes right back to the *Discourse on Metaphysics* and the *Correspondence with Arnauld*. I think that the meaning is as follows.

When he ascribes perception to a monad he means that each total state of the monad has a number of different features which are not separable or independent, and that each different feature corresponds to, and so represents, the contemporary state of a different one of the other monads. I think that the auditory field of a person who is listening to an orchestra composed of many different instruments playing simultaneously illustrates Leibniz's idea. But we must remember that normal human sense-perception is a very advanced kind of perception, which can happen only in the higher monads, just as deliberate conscious striving for an end is a very advanced kind of appetition.

Leibniz's general theory of representation may be expressed by the following symbolic scheme. Suppose that there was a set of n monads $M_1, M_2, \ldots, M_n$. Let M_r and M_s be two typical monads of the set. Let us denote the total state of M_r at a certain moment t by m_r^t, and the total state of M_s at the same moment by m_s^t. Then in m_r^t there will be a certain factor m_{r1}^t which corresponds to the contemporary total state m_1^t of M_1. There will be a certain other feature m_{r2}^t which corresponds to the contemporary total state m_2^t of M_2. And so on for the rest. The same remarks will apply *mutatis mutandis* to any other monad such as M_s. So we can write

$$m_r^t = f_r \left(m_{r1}^t, m_{r2}^t, \ldots, m_{rs}^t, \ldots, m_{rn}^t \right)$$

$$m_s^t = f_s \left(m_{s1}^t, m_{s2}^t, \ldots, m_{sr}^t, \ldots, m_{sn}^t \right)$$

with similar equations for each of the n monads. Here the letters f_r, f_s, etc. astride the bracket in each case represent the characteristic mode of combination in each monad of the various factors into a single total state. The whole history of the monad M_r will be a continuous series of such total states as m_r^t, producing each other without any influence from outside in accordance with the law of development which God impressed on the monad at its creation, and in consequence of the active force of appetition with which he endowed it.

Now Leibniz held that the number of monads must be infinite in order to explain the apparent continuity of ostensibly material objects.

[1] [G., VI, 608-9. Loemker, 644.]

Also he held that in *each* monad at any given moment the contemporary states of *all* other monads are represented. As he puts it: 'At every moment each monad mirrors the whole universe from its own special point of view.'[1] Therefore our group of n monads must include all the monads that there are, and the number will be infinite. So the total state of any monad at any moment will be infinitely complex. But the complexity does not consist of an infinite number of parts, which could conceivably be separated, like the bits in a jig-saw puzzle picture. It consists in an infinite number of inseparable superimposed *features* or modifications. If we want a physical analogy, the following may be useful. We can think of the total state of a monad at any moment as like the pattern of ripples on a pond, produced by the several ripples emanating from each of a number of stones dropped simultaneously into various parts of the pond at some date in the past.

I suspect that Leibniz's real reason for holding that each monad mirrors the contemporary state of all the others is the following. Everything in the universe appears to be influenced to some extent by everything else. E.g. every ostensible material particle is ostensibly attracted gravitationally by every other. Now really there is no matter and no interaction. But we have to account for the appearance of universal interaction between all the ostensible matter in the universe. Leibniz's solution is to say that what underlies the *appearance* of universal and mutual *interaction* is the *fact* of universal and mutual *representation*.

There is another complication to be considered. Leibniz held, not only that each total state of a monad mirrors the *contemporary* total states of all the *other* monads, but also that it mirrors in a very confused way every one of its *own past and future states*. He seems to have thought that this followed from the Predicate-in-Notion Principle and the fact that all causation is purely immanent. At every moment the monad must in some sense bear traces of all its past and traces of all its future, if it is to develop spontaneously in accordance with the plan laid down for it by God at its creation. We must therefore introduce into our formula a reflexive factor to symbolize the monad's representation at each moment of its states at all other moments. I shall symbolize this peculiar factor in the state of monad M_r at moment t by μ_{rr}^t. Thus our formulae finally become

$$m_r^t = f_r\ (\mu_{rr}^t;\ m_{r1}^t,\ m_{r2}^t,\ \ldots,\ m_{rs}^t,\ \ldots)$$

$$m_s^t = f_s\ (\mu_{ss}^t;\ m_{s1}^t,\ m_{s2}^t,\ \ldots,\ m_{sr}^t,\ \ldots)$$

[1] [G., VI, 618. Loemker, 649.]

If we think of Leibniz's theory in terms of modern physics we find that it is oversimplified in at least two respects. (1) It presupposes that heat, light, sound, etc. take no time to travel, i.e. that all the ostensible effects which one remote ostensible body has on another follow instantaneously on their ostensible causes. If we are to allow for the facts we shall have to say that the state of a monad at any moment t mirrors the states of other monads at earlier instants. We shall have to add that the time-lag in each case is correlated with the ostensible distance between the place where the one ostensible body was when it ostensibly sent out the influence and the place where the other ostensible body is when it ostensibly receives the influence. (2) Leibniz's theory also seems to ignore the existence of what appears to us as retarding and disturbing media between ostensible bodies. It is stated as if what appears to be the medium through which light, sound, etc. appear to travel from one ostensible body to another were always clear and homogeneous. If it is not, something in the state of each monad must be allowed for what common sense would describe as the effects of the transmitting medium. Leibniz would no doubt say that what we take to be a corporeal medium, e.g. glass, water, air, etc. must in fact consist of swarms of living creatures each composed of a dominant monad and an organism of subordinate monads. But the fact would remain that they are mirrored in a very different way from other monads, and that they appear to influence in a peculiar way the way in which other monads are mirrored.

4.2 Confusion

Leibniz ascribes to every monad a certain determinable quality which he calls 'Confusion'. We have seen that the total state of any monad at any moment must in fact be infinitely differentiated. For it contains a different modification corresponding to the contemporary state of every other monad, and the number of other monads is infinite. It also contains a modification corresponding to every one of its own past and future states, and the number of these will be infinite, since time is continuous. Now a monad is confused in so far as its total state at any moment contains modifications which it fails to recognize and distinguish. Leibniz used certain well-known psychological facts to show that the total state of any human mind, even at its most wakeful and attentive moments, contains factors which it fails to discriminate. If so, there is no difficulty in believing that monads below the level of human minds are habitually much more confused than human minds.

It is not so obvious why he should have been sure that created minds above the human level, e.g. those of angels, must all have some degree of confusion. I think that he probably postulated this in order that every created mind, however exalted, should differ in kind from God's mind. However that may be, it is certain that he held that every monad has *some* degree of confusion at *every* stage of its history. He seems to have held that no two monads can have precisely the same degree of confusion at the same moment. But the degree of confusion in a given monad may vary very much from time to time. This is illustrated by the difference between a human mind when fully awake and attentive, and the same kind when drowsy or drugged. Again I take it that the *distribution* of confusion within a monad might vary even if the total degree of it remained the same. At one moment a man is specially attending, e.g., to certain items in his usual field and at another he is specially attending to others. If Leibniz is right he is in some sense aware at every moment of everything in the universe and of his whole past and his whole future. This shift of attention must mean that some parts of his total experiences which were clear have become confused, and that others which were confused have become clear.

It will be remembered that Leibniz distinguishes in every monad two inseparable factors, viz. a substantial form or entelechy and stuff or *materia prima*. We can now identify each of these factors. The entelechy-factor is the activity which is characteristic of the monad, i.e. its activity of perceiving and striving. The stuff-factor is the internal limitation to which this inherent and incessant activity is more or less subjected at every moment in every monad. It is that which gives rise to confusion. We must remember that all the mental limitations, such as drowsiness, laziness, etc., which we commonly ascribe to the body, must, if Leibniz's denial of transeunt causation be accepted, be ascribed to something within the mind itself. It is this something within a monad, which limits and hampers its natural activities, that constitutes its stuff or *materia prima*.

4.3 Point of View

Leibniz holds that each monad at any moment has a certain peculiar quality which he calls its *Point of View*. No two monads at the same moment have the same point of view. But the point of view of a monad may alter in course of time, and so it may happen that a certain monad may acquire a certain point of view which formerly belonged to another monad. In a certain sense it may be said that the total external object perceived by any monad is the same as that perceived by any other monad, viz. the sum-total of all the monads. But, apart from the fact, already noted, that no two monads perceive this common object at any moment with the same total degree of confusion or with the same distribution of confusion, there is the further difference that they perceive it from different points of view. This doctrine goes right back to the *Discourse on Metaphysics*, and Leibniz never gave it up.

I think that this doctrine is designed to fit the following important facts. (1) Ostensible bodies appear to stand in various spatial relations to each other. These ostensible spatial relations sometimes remain constant for a while and sometimes change continuously. (2) The influences which ostensible bodies appear to exert on each other through gravitation, heat, electricity, etc. vary with their ostensible spatial relations to each other. (3) If an observer views a certain set of ostensible bodies, their apparent shapes and sizes vary in a systematic way with the ostensible spatial relations between them and the observer's ostensible body. This may be called the 'phenomenon of perspective'. It is illustrated also when we have an optical apparatus, such as a camera or a system of screens on which shadows are cast, instead of a human observer. Leibniz had to account for these systematically coordinated phenomena in terms of his own theory, which denies the reality of bodies and of relations.

His solution is to ascribe to each monad at every moment a certain determinable quality Q. This is called *Point of View*. Suppose that two very small ostensible bodies A and B appear to stand at a certain moment in a certain spatial relation to each other. The monads which are misperceived at t as the particle A then have values of Q which all cluster closely round a certain mean value q_A. The monads which are misperceived at t as the particle B then have values of Q which cluster closely round a certain other mean value q_B. The real basis of the apparent spatial relation is the difference in these two values q_A and q_B. In general the precise way in which the state of monad M_r at a given moment t is mirrored in another monad M_s depends jointly on q_r^t and q_s^t, the points of view of the two monads at that moment. That is the real basis of the phenomena of perspective and of the appearance of effects which vary with relative position.

5 Pre-established Harmony

According to Leibniz the fact which underlies the appearance of universal interaction between finite substances is that the total state of each monad at each moment is infinitely complex, and each different factor in it represents the contemporary total state of a different one of the remaining monads. Now, in consequence of his denial of the possibility of interaction between different substances, he has to hold that the state of each monad at each moment is completely determined by the immediately preceding state of *that* same monad in accordance with a *purely immanent* causal law. Why then should there be any correspondence at all between various monads, to say nothing of a complete one-to-one correlation between the state of each and the contemporary states of all the rest?

Since they were all created simultaneously by God, it is natural to connect this constant correlation between their contemporary states at all later moments with their common origin. Leibniz rejects the crude Occasionalist view that God continually interferes in the course of the world and directly produces a state β in substance *B* when he notices that a state α has occurred in substance *A*. This, he thinks, would be quite inconsistent with the wisdom and dignity of God. And, in any case, science and philosophy ought not to postulate a special action of God at every instant to account for ordinary routine natural phenomena.

Leibniz therefore puts forward the following theory. Anyone who admits the existence of a creative God must admit that he created each monad with certain dispositional properties and in a certain initial occurrent state. Suppose one accepts Leibniz's general theories of causation and substance. Then one will also have to admit that God gave to each monad the power and the tendency to develop spontaneously all its future states in succession according to the initial plan, without any interaction with other things and without any further special action by God. All that we need to suppose further is that God created each monad with such dispositional properties and in such an initial occurrent state that the contemporary subsequent states of all would correspond at each instant down to the minutest detail. So we have the one miracle of a co-ordinated creation without needing any subsequent miracles of interference. This is the doctrine of the *Pre-established Harmony*.

If the denial of transeunt causation were based upon the denial of relations in general, or even on the denial of relations between different substances, it would hardly be consistent to supplement it with the Pre-established Harmony. For the latter plainly presupposes temporal relations between total states of different monads, since it talks of the correlation of their *contemporary* states. It also presupposes relations of point-to-point correlation between the various distinguishable factors in the contemporary total states of different monads. But, as I have said, I do not believe that Leibniz's ground for denying the possibility of transeunt causation was his general principle of denying the reality of relations.

6 The three kinds of monad

All monads have all the properties which I have been describing. In addition, they all have the property of being ingenerable and indestructible by ordinary natural processes, because they are simple in the sense of not being composed of a plurality of coexisting parts. But Leibniz holds that they fall into three great classes, which form an ascending hierarchy. He calls these *Bare Monads*, *Animal Souls*, and *Rational Souls or Spirits*.

A *Bare Monad* is unable to discriminate the various features in its total state at any moment. It has no conscious memory of its past states and no conscious anticipation of its future states. It has therefore only completely unconscious perception and completely blind appetition. Ostensibly corporeal substances are certain aggregates of bare monads.

An *Animal Soul* has some degree of discrimination. It also has some degree of what Leibniz here calls 'memory'. But he does not mean by this personal recollection of particular events in its past history. He means what psychologists call 'retentiveness' and 'power of forming associations'. In consequence of this the mode of behaviour of an animal soul may be modified by past experiences in the sense that it may acquire 'conditioned responses'. Such monads are the souls of cats and dogs and oysters, and so on.

A *Rational Soul or Spirit* has, in addition to the properties possessed by an animal soul and a bare monad, the following further properties, which put it in a unique position in the universe. It has self-consciousness, and therefore can remember past events in its life. It can also imagine possible future states of affairs and strive deliberately to bring them about or to prevent them from being actualized. It has knowledge of necessary truths, such as the laws of logic and arithmetic, and can make deductive and inductive inferences. It also has knowledge of God and of categories, like cause and substance. Lastly, it is aware of the differences between right and wrong, good and evil, and is morally responsible; and it has the special desires and emotions which are bound up with moral cognition. Such monads are human souls and the souls of angels.

Within each of these classes there is a continuous series of monads differing in degree of confusion. On certain occasions and for limited periods a rational soul may become as confused as an animal soul normally is. This happens, e.g., to our souls when we faint or go to sleep. It almost certainly happens immediately after death. But that abnormal degree of confusion cannot last indefinitely, for a rational soul has to be restored to a state of comparative clearness at latest by the Last Judgment in order to recognize the justice of the verdict upon its past life and thereafter to enjoy its reward in Heaven or suffer its punishment in Hell.

No monad could pass from one of these classes to a higher one without a miracle, for they differ in kind. A bare monad lacks certain innate powers which an animal soul has, and an animal soul lacks certain innate powers which a rational soul has.

7 The real foundation of the various bodily phenomena

An ostensibly corporeal substance appears to have properties which fall into four classes, viz. sensible, geometrical, kinematic, and dynamical. By 'sensible qualities' I mean colour, heat and cold, taste, smell, etc. By 'geometrical qualities' I mean shape, size, and position. By 'kinematic properties' I mean motion of various kinds and rest. By 'dynamic properties' I mean impenetrability, inertial quiescence, inertial self-propagation, and forces or energies of various kinds such as that possessed by a moving bullet or a compressed spring.

7.1 Sensible qualities

Leibniz, like practically all the scientists and philosophers of any importance at that time, held that, if there are bodies, they are not really coloured, hot, etc., independently of human or animal percipients. And he held that, at the first move at any rate, the real independent basis of the phenomena of colour, temperature, etc. is the minute structure of bodies and the motions of their minute particles. At this level Leibniz would say that, when a person perceives something as red, he is perceiving confusedly a very large number of very similar minute motions in a very short period. The aggregate of these is perceived confusedly because each separate motion is so small and lasts for so short a time and because they are all so much alike. Consequently, though each is perceived, one's perception of each is unconscious, and so the perception of the whole aggregate of them is confused. Somehow this makes one perceive the object as coloured, although nothing is in fact coloured. Of course this cannot be Leibniz's ultimate view, since according to him there are really no motions to perceive whether confusedly or distinctly. But it suffices to show that we can confine our attention to the geometrical, kinematic, and dynamical properties of ostensible bodies, i.e. to those which scientists ascribe to them.

7.2 Geometrical properties

The real basis of the appearance of geometrical properties is the property of monads which he calls *Point of View*. It seems to me that Leibniz makes statements in different parts of his writings which are difficult to reconcile with each other. In the *Letters to de Volder* he says in one place that a monad has a 'certain ordered relation of coexistence to other things, in consequence of the machine which it dominates, i.e. a certain kind of position within extension, although it is not possible to assign it to a *point*.'[1] In his letter of 21 July 1707 to des Bosses he says that a simple substance, though it has no extension, has position which is the foundation of extension.[2] But in a later letter of 26 May 1712 he definitely asserts that monads do not have real positions relative to each other.[3] The ground given is that each is, as it were, a separate world, and that they are correlated with each other only through the Pre-established Harmony and by no other connexion. The statement in the letter to de Volder suggests that monads are spatially interrelated only indirectly through the organisms which they dominate. But, since the organism of a monad itself consists entirely of subordinate monads, this only shifts the problem from the dominant monads to the subordinate monads. And in any case, in Leibniz's complete theory, each subordinate monad is in its turn a dominant monad in respect of others which constitute its organism. I think that the remark quoted may be concerned only with the rather special question 'In what sense can you say that a man's soul is located somewhere within his body?' and is not intended to apply generally. The extreme negative statement in the letter of 26 May 1712 to des Bosses is consistent with, and perhaps a necessary consequence of, Leibniz's denial of relations between different substances. If there can be no relations there can be no spatial relations; and, if all position is relative, it cannot be literally true that one monad has a position relatively to another.

[1] [G., II, 253. Loemker, 531.]
[2] [G., II, 339.]
[3] [G., II, 444. Loemker, 602.]

I am inclined to think that the consistent view for Leibniz to take might be summarized as follows:

(1) What appears to a human being as a finite continuous body is really a set of bare monads of the following kind. (a) The points of view of all the monads in the set fall within certain limits. That is why the set is perceived as a finite body with a definite spatial boundary. (b) Every possible point of view within these limits belongs to some monad in the set. It is because of this, and because the possible points of view constitute a continuous manifold like the various possible shades of colour, e.g., that the set is perceived as a continuously extended and endlessly divisible object.

(2) Suppose that what is perceived as body A is perceived as standing in a certain spatial relation to what is perceived as a separate body B. What is perceived as body A is really a certain set α of monads such as I have been describing; and what is perceived as body B is really a certain other set β of monads such as I have been describing. The basis of the fact that A is perceived as at a distance from B is that the point of view of every monad in set α differs by a finite degree from that of every monad in set β. This might be compared with the differences, e.g., between a light shade of blue and a dark shade of blue. According to the amount and kind of difference between the points of view of monads in α and the points of view of monads in β, A will be perceived as more or less distant from B. Differences in ostensible direction could be dealt with on similar lines, but we should have to introduce three or more groups of monads each of which is misperceived as a body.

If this is the kind of thing that Leibniz had in mind the following points may be noted. (1) When I discussed the controversy about space and time between Leibniz and Clarke I said that ultimately Leibniz could not consistently hold a relational theory. He must hold that the real basis of the phenomenon of spatial position is certain pure qualities in the substance which appear to stand in spatial relations to each other. It now appears that the pure qualities are the points of view of the monads in those groups which are misperceived as extended and spatially interrelated bodies.

(2) The question remains: Why should we not take what Johnson would call the adjectival form of the theory of absolute position, and simply identify points of view with perfectly determinate forms of a determinable quality of absolute spatial position? It seems to me that it is only a question of the usage of words whether we will do this or not.

7.3 Kinematic properties

Suppose that what appears as a body A is perceived to move relatively to what appears as body B without any change in the size or shape of either. What appears as A will be a group α of monads such as I have described, and what appears as B will be another such group β of monads. The real foundation of the appearance of relative motion is that the points of view of the monads in α, or of the monads in β, or of both, are changing in a certain characteristic way. Let us confine our attention to α. The points of view of all monads in α must be changing in such a way that the *difference* in point of view between any two of them remains unaltered. Otherwise α would appear as a body which is changing in size or in shape or is disintegrating into a number of separate bodies. The situation might be compared to two sounds which are both changing in absolute pitch, but keep the same relative pitch. Similar remarks apply to the changes in the points of view of the monads in set β. Lastly, there must be a difference in the rate of change of point of view between the monads of group α and the monads of group β. Otherwise α and β would be perceived as two bodies A and B which are at rest relatively to each other.

Here again we must remark that, although Leibniz has argued against Newton that all motion is relative, he must in a sense deny this. The appearance of a change of spatial relation between bodies must be a phenomenon founded upon changes of pure quality in the monads of the groups which are misperceived as those bodies. Whether you choose to call these changes of point of view 'absolute motions' or not seems to me to be largely a matter of words. They are not absolute motions in the sense in which Newton would have interpreted that phrase. For Newton's interpretation involves the substantival theory of Space which Leibniz has rejected. But there seems to be no good reason to refuse to call them absolute motions in the Johnsonian sense, which involves only that position is a pure quality and not a relational property.

7.4 Dynamical properties

In dealing with Leibniz's Dynamics we saw that he argued successfully against Descartes that the notion of corporeal substance involves much beside geometrical and kinematic properties. It involves in addition impenetrability and inertia, which Leibniz lumps together as *primitive passive force*, and various kinds of energy which he lumps together as *primitive active force.* The question now is: 'What corresponds, in the monads of a group α which is perceived as a body *A*, to those various dynamical properties which appear to belong to the body *A*?'

In his letter of 19 January 1706 to de Volder Leibniz states quite explicitly that force, in so far as it is thought of as a property of extended massive bodies, is not something that exists independently of an observer. It is a phenomenon founded upon certain real properties of monads, just as extension, motion, and mass themselves are. Nothing exists in its own right except percipients and their perceptions and anything that may be involved in these.[1]

Leibniz holds that the real factor in monads which gives rise to the appearance of impenetrability and inertia in ostensible bodies is the element of confusion in them. In the individual monad this is the factor which limits its powers of perception and discrimination and explicit memory and anticipation. When a number of monads constitute a group of such a kind as to appear as an extended object the element of confusion in them makes that object appear to be impenetrable and inert.

The real factor in monads which gives rise to the appearance of active forces or energies in ostensible bodies is the element of appetition in them. In the letter to de Volder which I quoted above he says that force (in the individual monad) is simply the ground of transition to new perceptions. When a number of monads constitute a group of such a kind as to appear as an extended object the element of appetition in them makes that object appear to be possessed of energy; either of the kinetic form, as when a massive body is in motion, or of various potential forms, as in a suspended weight, a compressed spring, and so on.

The following quotation from Leibniz's *Remarks on Bayle's Article Rorarius* seems to me to be interesting in this connexion: 'Matter is not capable of maintaining itself in circular motion, for this motion is not simple enough for it to be able to remember. It remembers only what happens to it at the last moment . . . i.e. it remembers the direction along the tangent' (i.e. to the circular course which it has been travelling) 'without having the gift of remembering the instruction which would be given to it to turn aside from that tangent. . . That is why an atom can only learn to go simply in a straight line, such is its stupidity and imperfection. The case is quite different with a soul or mind. . . It remembers (confusedly of course) all its previous states and is affected by them. It not only holds its direction . . . but it holds also

[1] [G., II, 281–2. Loemker, 539.]

the law of the changes of direction.'[1] In this quotation one must substitute for 'matter' and 'atom' the bare monads which when perceived in suitable groupings appear as a body or as an extended particle. (Leibniz makes the same point in his *Second Answer to Bayle*.)[2]

The following comments may be made on this part of Leibniz's theory of monads:

(1) I think it is a mistake to lump together impenetrability and inertia. They are so utterly different in kind that it seems implausible to ascribe the appearance of both of them to a single factor in the individual monads, viz. their confusion.

(2) I think it is a mistake to lump together under the head of 'inertia' the two logically separable characteristics which I have distinguished as *inertial quiescence* and *inertial self-propagation*. It may be plausible to associate the reluctance of a body to be set in motion with the passive features of confusion in the monads. But surely its tendency to maintain itself in motion with the same velocity and in the same direction should be associated with the active factor of appetition in the monads.

(3) Even if these mistakes were avoided, the associations in question seem very fanciful. No doubt we do talk of 'mental inertia', of 'force and persistence of willing', and so on. But the analogy of these to inertia and energy respectively in corporeal substances seems very slight.

(4) It will be useful to notice here that Leibniz uses each of the two technical terms *materia prima* and *materia secunda* in two different senses, which might be called a phenomenal and a metaphysical sense. When he is writing primarily as a physicist he uses *materia prima* to mean corporeal substance considered simply as having extension, impenetrability, inertia, and mobility. This is an abstraction, for all bodies have also inherent active forces or energies. In the metaphysical sense *materia prima* is that factor of confusion which is present in each individual monad. It is the correlate of its entelechy, i.e. of its positive active powers of perception and appetition. He uses *materia secunda* in the phenomenal sense to mean corporeal substances regarded as extended, mobile, impenetrable, inert, and the seat of various active forces. He is particularly liable to use it of the substances which make up an animal body considered simply as a physical object and without reference to the soul which animates it. In the metaphysical sense *materia secunda* means any collection of bare monads which appear as a body. In particular it means the collection of subordinate monads

---

[1] [G., IV, 543-4.]
[2] [G., IV, 554-71. Loemker, 574-85.]

which appear as the body of an animal, considered in abstraction from the dominant monad which is its soul.

(5) It is important to notice that, on Leibniz's theory, the appearance of corporeal substance depends on a double confusion, viz. in the object and in the subject. (a) A set of monads will not be perceived by any mind as a corporeal substance unless *they* are all extremely confused. (b) A mind will not perceive any set of very confused monads as a corporeal substance unless *it* is itself somewhat confused. If the percipient were free from confusion, he would perceive such a group correctly, viz. as an infinite collection of very confused minds whose points of view are all confined within certain limits. No doubt, e.g., God perceives those sets of monads which we misperceive as bodies. And no doubt he knows that we misperceive them as bodies. But he certainly does not misperceive them as bodies himself. He perceives them correctly as groups of confused monads.

8 Theory of organisms

It will be best to take Leibniz's doctrine of organisms in two stages. We will first talk as if organisms really were bodies, as they appear to be. Then we will take account of the fact that what appear to be bodies are really certain collections of low-grade monads.

8.1 General account

(1) An organism is said to be a 'natural machine'. In the *Système Nouveau* it is said that a natural machine differs from an artificial one in at least the following three respects.[1] (a) It has an infinite number of organs. (b) Every part of it, however small, is itself a machine. (c) It always remains the same machine, being merely compressed or folded when it seems to be destroyed. He adds that the presence of a soul animating a natural machine gives a unity (analogous to that of a human individual) to which there is no analogy in the case of an artificial machine. In the *Letters to de Volder* it is repeated that an organism has an infinite number of organs, and two reasons are given. One is that it requires them in order to be able to express in its own way the whole universe. The other is in order to contain at every moment traces of all its past and all its future history.[2]

An organism neither begins nor ceases in the course of nature. It

[1] [G., IV, 482. Loemker, 456.]
[2] [G., II, 251. Loemker, 529–30.]

merely unfolds and takes up and organizes new material when it seems to be generated; and it merely closes up and sheds a great deal of material rather rapidly when it seems to die. When we say that the same organism has persisted throughout the whole of history, we must remember that the sameness of an organism does not imply that any part of it, however small, has always been and will always continue to be a part of it. The characteristic feature of an organism is that it is constantly taking in material from outside and organizing it into itself, and constantly shedding material which formerly was part of it.

Leibniz takes it to be certain that every organism is animated by a soul or something analogous to a soul; and that every soul or substance analogous to a soul always animates an organism. In the *Letters to des Bosses* Leibniz says that it is not *necessary* that every organism should be animated, and conversely that it is not *necessary* that a soul should animate an organism. But it would be contrary to God's wisdom to have created an organism without a soul to animate it, and it would be contrary to the order of things for him to create a soul without an organism for it to animate.[1]

Though the identity of an organism through time does not depend on its retaining any particular bit of material as a part throughout its whole history, it is very closely connected with being animated by the same soul throughout its whole history. A soul persists in a quite different way and for quite different reasons from an organism. A soul is simple, while an organism consists of an infinite number of simultaneous parts; and a soul is ingenerable and incorruptible because of its internal simplicity. Suppose that a living organism is cut up. Then that part, and only that part, which continues to be animated by the soul which formerly animated the whole, can be said to be the same organism as that whole. Then, again, a soul which has been animating an organism never begins to animate another organism which is not continuous with the former. That would involve *transmigration*, which Leibniz rejects, instead of *transformation*, which he accepts.

Suppose we start with a living creature or animal, which we will denote by A. It might, e.g., be a certain cat. It will consist of an organism O together with a soul S which animates it. Now, according to Leibniz the organism O is itself an aggregate of many living creatures, which we will denote by $A_1, A_2, \ldots, A_r, \ldots$ Each of these, e.g. A_r, consists of an organism O_r together with a soul S_r which animates it. This goes on indefinitely. E.g. O_r, the organism of the second-order living creature A_r, is itself an aggregate of many living creatures, which

[1] [G., II, 378.]

we can denote by $A_{r_1}, A_{r_2}, \ldots, A_{r_s}, \ldots$ Each of these, e.g. A_{r_s}, consists of an organism O_{r_s} together with a soul S_{r_s} which animates it.
This hierarchy goes downwards without end. We might think of A_1,
$A_2, \ldots, A_r$, etc. as cellular animals, provided we think of each cell as
animated by a soul. Each cell would then be the body of a cellular
animal. We must therefore regard it as consisting of cellular animals
of a lower order, each with a soul and a body. And so on. This hierarchy does not go upwards without end. There is, e.g., no reason to
believe that a cat is one of the animals in the organism of some living
creature which stands to it in the kind of relation in which it stands to
one of the cellular animals in its own organism.

The soul which animates a body perceives or represents *primarily*
what happens in that body. But the body represents from its own standpoint and in its own way everything else in the universe, and so the soul,
in representing what happens in its own body, represents indirectly
what is happening everywhere in the universe. Conversely everything
that happens in a soul is represented by modifications of the body which
it animates. Even in abstract reasoning the symbols are something
bodily, and they, and our operations with them, represent processes
of abstract thinking in our souls. The tendencies in the soul towards
new thoughts correspond to the tendencies in the body to new internal
modifications and motions.

As regards the question whether the soul can be said to be located
in the body which it animates, Leibniz's statements seem somewhat
ambiguous. In the *Letters to de Volder* he says that a ruling monad has
'a certain ordered relation of coexistence to other things, i.e. a certain
kind of position within extension' *in consequence of* the organism which
it dominates. But he adds that it is not possible to assign it to a *point*.[1]
In the *Letters to des Bosses* he reiterates the statement that a soul cannot
be regarded as occupying a geometrical point.[2] Yet, at another place
in the same series of letters, he says that, although a simple substance
has no extension, yet 'it has position, which is the foundation of
extension'.[3] Nevertheless, he says in another letter to des Bosses that
monads do not have real positions relatively to each other. He gives
as his reason that 'each is, as it were, a separate world', and they are
correlated with each other only through the correlation between their
contemporary total states. There is neither nearness nor remoteness
between monads, and it is equally meaningless to say of a monad that

[1] [G., II, 253. Loemker, 531.]
[2] [G., II, 370. Loemker, 598.]
[3] [G., II, 339.]

it is confined to a point or that it is spread out in space.[1] Lastly, I will quote a curious passage from his letter of 30 April 1709 to des Bosses: 'I do not deny that there is a certain real metaphysical union between the soul and the organic body, which justifies one in saying that the soul *really is* in the body. But, since this cannot be explained from the phenomena and does not make any difference to them, I cannot explain more distinctly in what it consists. It is enough to say that it is bound up with the correspondence.'[2] (I take this to mean the specially intimate correspondence between what goes on in a soul and what goes on simultaneously in the body which it animates.)

(2) I think that this is about all that one can say of Leibniz's views about the nature of organisms and the relation of animation between a certain soul and a certain organism, when one talks as if there really were bodies. We must now combine it with his doctrine that there really are no bodies, and that what we misperceive as a body is really a collection of very confused minds. The complete theory is that there really are organisms and that every monad really animates an organism, but that an organism is not really a body.

The theory might be put as follows. Each monad m is associated at any moment t with a certain group of lower monads which we can denote by g_{mt}. If we consider two moments t and t' in the history of m the contents of g_{mt} and $g_{mt'}$ are never exactly the same. If t and t' are remote from each other g_{mt} and $g_{mt'}$ may contain no monads in common. But, if t and t' are very near together, the contents of g_{mt} and $g_{mt'}$ will as a rule very considerably overlap. If t is a moment shortly before and t' a moment shortly after the death of an ordinary macroscopic animal, such as a cat, $g_{mt'}$ will consist of a comparatively small selection out of g_{mt}. We call m the *dominant* or *ruling* monad of g_{mt}; we call g_{mt} the *organism* of m at t; and we say that the monads in g_{mt} are *subordinate* to m at t. The state of m at t corresponds more closely to the states of the monads in g_{mt} than to the contemporary states of other monads. It represents the states of the monads in g_{mt} directly. It represents the contemporary states of other monads only *indirectly*, in consequence of the fact that their contemporary states are represented in the monads of g_{mt}. There is some rather close connexion between the point of view of m at t and the points of view of the monads in g_{mt}. Lastly, g_{mt} is a group of such a kind that it is perceived by m itself and other confused monads as a *body*. It is perceived by m itself as its *own body*, partly (in the case of men and the higher animals) by sight and touch, but more intimately by what we call

[1] [G., II, 451. Loemker, 604.] [2] [G., II, 371. Loemker, 598.]

'bodily feeling', 'kinaesthetic sensation', and so on. It is perceived by other monads *only* by sight or touch or something analogous to these; so they perceive it as a *foreign* body. Owing to the special similarity between the point of view of *m* and the points of view of the monads in g_{mt} there is a sense in saying that the soul is located within the body which it animates. But to say this is at best only phenomenally true; and even in phenomenal terms it would be incorrect to say that the soul is located at a certain geometrical point in its body.

I think that Leibniz would hold that all the monads in g_{mt} are more confused than its ruling monad *m*. Now each monad in g_{mt} also rules an organism of subordinate monads, each of these rules an organism of subordinate monads, and so on without end. It would follow that there is no last term in the series of more and more confused monads. It would also follow that the total number of monads at each level of confusion increases as we go down the scale.

Though every monad rules some organism, not every monad is a member of the organism of some higher monad. Human souls, e.g., are certainly not members of the organisms of higher monads; each human soul comes at the head of a descending hierarchy of monads. So the universe as a whole is not an organism. And of course there are many ostensible bodies which are not the appearances of an organism. The group of monads, e.g., which appears as a stone is not the organism of any monad. But it is wholly composed of living creatures, each with its ruling monad and its organism of subordinate monads. It might be compared to a swarm of gnats misperceived as a cloud.

Supposing this, or something like it, to be Leibniz's theory, we can ask what were his reasons for holding it. As usual he was, I think, trying to do justice to a number of empirical facts consistently with certain general metaphysical principles, such as the denial of transeunt causation.

(1) I think that the panorganic theory was first introduced in order to save the reality of corporeal substance by finding intrinsic natural units in it. This introduced, as a consequence, a whole array of minds or souls below the level of human or ordinary animal souls, because Leibniz thought that every living organism must be animated by something akin to a soul.

(2) At that stage the number of organisms would be infinite, and they would form a kind of descending hierarchy, for the following reason at any rate. Leibniz held that the existence of empty volumes within the world is incompatible with the wisdom of God. Therefore the gaps within and between organisms of any given order must be

occupied by smaller organisms; the gaps within and between these must be occupied by still smaller organisms, and so on without end. (Cf. Leibniz's illustration of filling spaces with a hierarchy of spheres.) This, however, would not explain why every organism must itself be *composed of organisms* and so on without end. For it is plainly one thing to say that the holes within and the gaps between organisms must always be occupied by other organisms, and another thing to say that each organism must itself be composed of other organisms.

(3) At a later stage Leibniz became persuaded by the argument from endless divisibility that the reality of corporeal substance could not be saved. No substance can really be extended, whether it is an animated organism or not. The only genuine substances are unextended and of the nature of minds or souls; and what we take to be a body must be a certain kind of collection of souls.

(4) If we accept this, we must interpret all other substances by analogy with our own souls, for these are the only simple substances with which we are acquainted. Now it is an empirical fact that each different *human* soul appears to be uniquely associated with a different human body, and the same appears to hold for all the higher animals. A human soul seems to affect and to be affected by foreign bodies and other souls only through the medium of its own body. And its perception of the rest of the world seems to be coloured by the nature of the processes in its own body, and to be a kind of perspective view with its own body as centre.

Leibniz generalized this to the principle that *every* different soul must stand in this unique kind of relation to a different living body. Since every simple substance is of the nature of a soul, it follows that every simple substance must animate something of the nature of a living body. But what we take to be a living body must itself consist entirely of simple substances, and therefore of things of the nature of souls. Therefore every monad in the organism of a given ruling monad must itself rule an organism of subordinate monads, and so on without end.

(5) When we say that a human soul perceives and acts upon the rest of the world by means of the body which it animates, we are thinking in terms of transeunt causation. We think, e.g., of a foreign body emitting light, of the light travelling to a human body and acting on its retina; of this setting up a disturbance in the optic nerve and eventually in a part of the brain; and of this finally producing a colour-sensation in the soul. But, on Leibniz's general principles, all this is only phenomenally true. Really there is no interaction between the group of monads which I perceive as the sun, e.g., and the group of

monads which I perceive as my body. Nor is there any interaction between the latter group and my soul. The facts underlying these phenomenally true, but metaphysically misleading, statements are facts about the correlation of contemporary states of monads in accordance with the Pre-established Harmony. But we must think of the correlation between the state of my soul at any moment and the contemporary states of the monads in my organism as being very different in principle from the correlation of the latter with the contemporary states of the monads in the group which I perceive as the sun. For, empirically, there is an enormous difference between the purely *physical transaction* which we describe as the emission of light from the sun to my eye and the consequent disturbance of my optic nerve and brain, and the *psycho-physiological transaction* which we describe as the production of a sensation in my mind by a disturbance in my brain. This must correspond to an important difference in the underlying facts; and that difference must be retained when we drop the fiction of causal transactions and substitute the reality of representation in accordance with the Pre-established Harmony.

8.2 Death and birth

We might be inclined to regard Leibniz's doctrine that no organism can begin or cease to exist in the course of nature as an extravagant fantasy. I do not think that this would be fair. We have to consider it in relation to the following four propositions. (1) Every living organism is animated by something of the nature of a soul. (2) Every soul is a simple substance. (3) No simple substance can begin or cease to exist except by a miracle. (4) Except by a miracle a soul cannot exist without an organism.

Take any animal which now exists, e.g. the present Trinity Combination Room cat. Since its ostensible body is a living organism it must be animated by a soul. Since that soul is a simple substance it cannot be destroyed by any natural process, and therefore not by the death of the cat. If, then, we do not assume that God miraculously annihilates it, it must persist after the death of the cat. But, if it persists, it must continue to animate *some* appropriate organism. Either this is continuous with the organism of the cat just before death or it is not. The latter supposition, which would be involved in the doctrine of transmigration, is contrary to the Principle of Continuity. So, unless we are willing to postulate miracles of one kind or another at the death of every animal, we are practically committed by Leibniz's various premisses to the doctrine that an organism, continuous with the organism which existed at the moment of death, persists after death and is animated by the same soul.

Similar remarks apply to the birth of the cat. Either its soul was miraculously created at the moment of conception or it existed beforehand. If it existed beforehand, it must have animated some kind of organism beforehand. If the Principle of Continuity is to be observed this organism must be continuous with that of the embryonic cat as it was just after conception. The empirical fact, at that time recently observed by microscopists, that spermatozoa are tiny living creatures, seemed to give detailed empirical support to Leibniz's theory of conception and gestation. We now know that, whatever the facts may be, they must be more complex than Leibniz supposed, since the embryo arises from the combination of an ovum from the female parent and a spermatozoon from the male parent. It appears therefore that a new organism arises from the blending of the two pre-existing organisms. On Leibniz's principles each of these would be animated by its own soul, and the new organism would be animated by its own soul. In theory, I suppose, one might hold either that the soul of the spermatozoon becomes that of the embryo, and that the soul of the ovum becomes a subordinate monad in the organism; or vice versa; or that the souls of both become subordinate to a third soul. The third alternative might lead to difficulties about the Principle of Continuity. Perhaps another possibility would be to hold that only the spermatozoon is an animated organism, and that the ovum is just an aggregate of monads which is not subordinate to any one ruling monad. In that case the soul of the embryo would, as on Leibniz's theory, be the soul of the spermatozoon. Either Leibniz's original theory or this amendment of it would have difficulty in accounting for the fact, which must have been as obvious to Leibniz as it is to us, that a child may take after its mother rather than its father in its *mental* characteristics.

8.2.1 The case of rational souls

Leibniz remarks in the *Letters to John Bernoulli* that his general doctrine about the souls and the organisms of living creatures below the human level is meant to leave open the question of the origin and destiny of rational souls.[1] They differ in several important respects from other monads. In particular the fact that they are self-conscious and have personal memory and a knowledge of good and evil and right and

[1] [G. M., III, 559–61.]

wrong makes it possible for them to be treated *justly* or *unjustly*. That question cannot arise in regard to animal souls and bare monads. In the *Système nouveau* Leibniz says explicitly that no change could happen to a spirit which would deprive it of its *moral* qualities.[1]

We must therefore consider specially what happens at the conception and the death of a human being. In the *Letters to Arnauld* Leibniz says that God creates rational souls in the course of history whenever he thinks fit.[2] I take this to mean that he creates a rational soul and subordinates the embryonic organism to it whenever a human being is conceived. In the *Letters to des Bosses*, which are much later, he wavers between this and another view. The other alternative is that the souls of human spermatozoa are, by nature, animal and not rational monads. At the conception of a human being God miraculously raises the one spermatozoon concerned to the rational level, and leaves the others as they were. In his letter of 30 April 1709 to des Bosses he mentions this theory.[3] He says that he prefers the theory that God creates a rational soul, although he thinks it unlikely that God creates new *non-rational* monads in the course of history. But in his letter of 31 July 1709 he says that it seems more fitting to suppose that, when a man is conceived, a certain animal soul is miraculously raised to the level of a rational soul than that all the souls of human spermatozoa are rational.[4] For the vastly greater proportion of them will never develop into human beings.

Thus it would seem that the alternatives contemplated by Leibniz may be classified as follows. (1) That the souls of human spermatozoa are rational, and that the development of a man at conception is exactly parallel to that of an animal at conception, the only difference being that the soul is rational in one case and merely animal in the other. (2) That the souls of human spermatozoa are not rational but are merely animal. This gives rise to two alternatives. (a) That, at the conception of a human being, God miraculously creates a rational soul and makes it dominant over the monads which have been the organism of one of the spermatozoa of the father. (b) That, at the conception of a human being, God miraculously raises the soul of the one spermatozoon concerned from the merely animal to the rational level. Thus both forms of the second alternative require a miracle at the conception of each human being, though it is a different kind of miracle in each of the two forms.

The disadvantage of alternative (1) is the waste and apparent in-

---

[1] [G., IV, 481. Loemker, 455.]   [2] [G., II, 100. Mason, 125.]
[3] [G., II, 371. Loemker, 598.]   [4] [G., II, 378.]

justice involved in the existence of myriads of rational souls which never get a chance to exercise their powers by dominating a macroscopic human organism. Its advantage is that it avoids miracles. On alternative (2a) there would seem to be the following difficulty. What becomes of the animal soul which dominated the spermatozoon which develops into a human body? Does it remain and continue to dominate? If so, the human being has two souls, one animal which it took over from the spermatozoon, and the other rational and specially created by God at conception. This is certainly not Leibniz's usual view, and it would lead to various awkward questions about the relations between the two souls. Alternative (2b) avoids this difficulty of two souls. It seems on the whole the best that Leibniz could adopt.

Leibniz says explicitly that the theory known as *Traducianism*, i.e. that the soul of the child is in some sense produced by and from the souls of both its parents, is nonsense.

The following remarks, all from the *Letters to des Bosses*, about the possibility of God creating monads in the course of history, are worth noting here. (1) God could at any time create a new monad without having to create a whole lot of subordinate monads to be its organism.[1] For he could make it the dominant monad of some group of pre-existing monads which were not the organism of any pre-existing monad. He could, e.g., make it the dominant monad of a group of monads which had previously appeared as an inorganic body, e.g. a stone. The stone would then become an animal. I assume that God would have to rearrange these pre-existing monads very considerably. And one would have, I suppose, in addition to the miracle of a new *simple substance* being created in the course of history, the miracle of a *new organism* being constructed in the course of history. (2) The creation of a new monad (or indeed of any finite number of them) would not, empirically speaking, increase the quantity of corporeal substance in the world. It would, Leibniz says, be 'like adding a point to a line'.[2] This is obviously correct. According to Leibniz, an ostensible body, however small it may appear to be, must be the appearance of an infinitely numerous group of monads. For, otherwise, it would not appear to be endlessly divisible into smaller adjoined extended parts.

I cannot find any very clear account in Leibniz of what happens to a human soul between the death of its ordinary body and the Day of Judgment. No doubt it continues to dominate a small selection of monads from the larger group which constituted its organism just before death. I suppose that it remains in a very confused state until the

[1] [G., II, 368.]　　　　　　　　　　[2] [ibid.]

Day of Judgment; that its organism then takes in numbers of other monads and would appear as a human body of normal size; and that it wakes up, regains its memories, and receives its appropriate reward or punishment which will go on thenceforth for ever.

There is one final remark to be made about the theory of the animated organism in general. It is almost impossible to state it or conceive it without assuming the reality of relations. An organism seems to be a group of monads interrelated in a very special way. And a ruling monad seems to be related to the monads in its organism in a very special way. Leibniz would have to say that all these relational statements are reducible to statements about pure qualities of the several monads concerned. But I find this very hard to accept.

9 Apparent interaction of body and mind

It will be as well to consider this problem in its historical setting. As far as I am aware, it did not exist for the Greeks or for the Scholastics. It begins with Descartes.

9.1 Historical background of the problem

(1) The question for Descartes may be put as follows: 'Granted that a human mind and the body which it animates are substances of different kinds interrelated in a peculiarly intimate way, how can events in the one produce or modify events in the other?' Descartes thought that the occurrence of rational speech and intelligent action proves conclusively that certain events in a person's mind do affect the movements of his bodily organs, and that the occurrence of organic sensations, emotions, and images proves conclusively that certain events in a person's body do affect the experiences of his mind.

The difficulty for him was two-fold. (a) It was difficult to see how an unextended mental substance, which had no fundamental property except cognition, and an unthinking material substance, which had no fundamental property but extension, could ever come to grips with each other. (b) If the mind affected the movements of the body it would add to the amount of motion in the world. But Descartes thought he could prove from the perfection of God that in all the changes of bodies the same aggregate quantity of motion is conserved.

Descartes's solution was to say that interaction between mind and body takes place *only* in human beings; that in them it takes place only at one point, viz. the pineal gland; and that even there it produces only a change in the direction of pre-existing motion without changing its total quantity. It acts as the points on a railway influence the direction of a train by deflecting it from one line to another.

(2) This solution gave little satisfaction. The next attempt was made by the Occasionalists, who were nearly all in the main disciples of Descartes. (a) The crudest form of Occasionalism is as follows. A person's mind and his body are two substances, but they cannot act on each other. God, being omnipotent, can act on both; and, being omniscient, he is aware of any event that takes place in either. Suppose that at a certain moment a volition to move his arm in a certain way arises in a certain man's mind. God notices this. And, in general, on such occasions he deliberately causes that man's arm to move in accordance with his volition. The apparent causation of a painful sensation in a man's mind by a pin puncturing his skin would be explained in a similar way. God notices that the pin is entering the skin, and as a rule he thereupon produces a painful sensation in the man's mind. (b) A much less crude form of Occasionalism was reached by Malebranche, through developing certain aspects of Descartes's theory of created substance. Descartes held that any finite substance needs, not only to be created in the first instance by God, but also to be continually re-created in order to keep it going from moment to moment. Malebranche thought that this makes each finite substance into a mere series of occurrents, each of which is directly and wholly due to God, and none of which is a state of any continuant. We say that a certain finite substance has persisted unchanged, or has altered in a certain way, or has ceased to exist, according to how God chooses to act from moment to moment in creating new occurrents. On this view there is no real interaction between any finite substance and any other. There is not even immanent causation between the successive states of the same finite substance. These are merely rules which God generally follows. If he continues a certain series in a certain way, he generally continues adjacent series in certain other correlated ways. So we say that a certain event in one substance causes certain other events in adjacent substances in accordance with a certain law.

(3) It will be seen that with Malebranche the problem has widened out from being a departmental problem of how a mind interacts with the body which it animates to being a general problem of how any finite substance interacts with any other. The next attempt at solution comes from Spinoza. He accepted Malebranche's conclusion that the so-called 'finite substances' of common sense are not genuine

continuants. According to him there can be one and only one genuine continuant. He applied this reasoning equally to minds and to bodies. But (a) he objected altogether to ascribing volition and deliberate action to God. (b) He thought it self-evident that every occurrent must inhere in some continuant. (c) He did not think that there is any incompatibility between an event or process being mental and its being material. On the contrary, he seems to have held that anything which had *either* of these properties would necessarily have *both*.

He therefore took the following view. There is one and only one continuant, viz. God. This is both mental and material; but it is neither a mind nor a body. Every so-called 'finite substance' is a more or less continuous and coherent series of occurrents in the one continuant. Its unity and persistence and self-identity are like those of a wave or a shadow. Apart from these differences, Spinoza's theory of the causation of one finite mode by another is not unlike Malebranche's occasionalism, except that it all happens necessarily and automatically and is not the result of volition on God's part. When one finite substance seems to produce or modify or destroy another by its own power, that is an illusion. The fact is that so much of the total energy of God ceases to be manifested in a certain way at a certain place and time, and it begins to be manifested in a certain other way or it becomes for a time latent. The sort of occasions on which this happens can be brought under rules, and these are the causal laws of nature.

As to the particular problem of the apparent interaction between a mind and the body which it animates, this has entirely altered for Spinoza. The mind and the body of a man or an animal are not two *substances*, for they are not substances at all and they are not even *two* occurrents. The man or animal is a mode or occurrent in the one substance God, and every mode necessarily has both bodily and mental characteristics exactly correlated with each other. For any bodily fact about the mode John Smith there is a corresponding mental fact about him, and vice versa. What we call 'John Smith's mind' is simply John Smith, considered as the subject of mental facts, without reference to the correlated bodily facts. What we call 'John Smith's body' is simply John Smith, considered as the subject of bodily facts, without reference to the correlated mental facts. It becomes nonsensical to talk of interaction here, for interaction implies two terms; and here there is only a single term, considered under two different, but precisely correlated, abstract headings.

There is one other characteristic doctrine of Spinoza's to be mentioned. Suppose that at a certain moment an individual A has an experience which we will denote by e_ψ, and that the bodily correlate of this is an event in his brain which we will denote by e_ϕ. Then, as we have said, e_ψ and e_ϕ are just one and the same psycho-physical event $e_{\psi\phi}$, considered respectively in its purely mental and its purely bodily aspects. But we must now add that Spinoza holds a very peculiar view as to the nature of the correlation between the two aspects of the single event $e_{\psi\phi}$. He holds that $e_{\psi\phi}$, considered in its purely mental aspect e_ψ, is a state of confused but direct acquaintance with itself considered in its purely bodily aspect e_ϕ. Thus e.g., to have a colour-sensation is to be acquainted in a confused way with that event in one's brain which is the bodily correlate of the experience.

9.2 Leibniz's solution

We come now to Leibniz. He was of course fully aware of the developments in the controversy since Descartes's time, and he put forward his own theories in view of the suggestions of Descartes, Malebranche, and Spinoza.

As regards Descartes he points out that the suggestion that the soul can change the direction of pre-existing motions in the body, but cannot add to the quantity of motion in the world, does not meet the real difficulty. By 'quantity of motion' Descartes meant the product of the mass of a body by its velocity taken without regard to direction or sign. He was mistaken in thinking that the sum-total of this is conserved in all dynamical transactions. But Leibniz substituted for the false principle of the *Conservation of Motion* the true principle of *Conservation of Momentum*. The momentum of a body in a given direction in a given straight line is defined as the product of its mass by the component of its velocity in that direction along that line. Thus momentum may be positive or negative according to the angle which the direction of a body's motion makes with the assigned direction. Leibniz recognized the fact that the total momentum of all the bodies in the world in any direction (when account is taken of sign) is constant. Now, if the soul were to alter the direction of the pre-existing motions even without altering the magnitude of the velocities, we should have a conflict with the Conservation of Momentum.

As regards Malebranche and the other Occasionalists Leibniz took the following line. They are right in saying that finite substances do not interact, and that every created substance is, in a sense, continually produced by God. But we ought not to be content with this. Occasionalism would involve continual miracles on the most trivial occasions, because it requires a *special* action of God on each particular occasion, instead of a *general* reference to the natures which God gave to created things at the beginning and which he has maintained ever since in them. God acts in general only by natural means. He puts into each thing that he creates the principle of its subsequent changes and the activity or energy required to carry out those changes in accordance with the principle.

As regards Spinoza, Leibniz held, for reasons which we have already considered, that there is a plurality of finite substances, and that there is no reason to hold that what we take to be finite substances are all occurrents in a single continuant. Again, he could not put the bodily and the mental aspects of the world on a level. Nothing could have certain of the features, e.g. endless divisibility, which bodies appear to have and which are part of the notion of a body. What we take to be bodies are really certain collections of low-grade minds which we mis-perceive as bodies because we are ourselves rather confused.

The difficulty which Descartes felt about the interaction of soul and body, viz. that they are so utterly unlike in nature, does not exist for Leibniz. Nor does the difficulty which Spinoza felt, viz. that soul and body are not two terms but are one and the same term considered under two different abstract headings. For Leibniz the ruling monad is one substance, and the monads which together constitute its organism are different substances of the same general character as itself (viz. minds), though of a lower order of clearness and intelligence. Nevertheless, Leibniz did in fact deny the possibility of interaction between *any* two finite substances, and he explained the appearance of such interaction by the hypothesis of *Pre-established Harmony*. We have already dealt with his views on these general questions, and it remains only to see how he applied the general principles to the particular case of a ruling monad and its organism.

All that remains of the old problem is this: 'What is really happening in the ruling monad and in the monads of its organism when we say that a person's mind voluntarily produces a certain movement of his body or that an event in his body produces a certain sensation in his mind?' Suppose, e.g., that I will to move my arm in a certain way and that it thereupon moves as I wish. My present volition must be caused entirely by something in the previous state of my soul. Its effects must consist entirely in certain later changes in my soul. E.g. the cause might be a feeling of discomfort and a belief that it would be advantageous to me to have my arm in the proposed new position. Now consider the same incident from the standpoint of my arm. What I perceive as my arm is in fact a certain set of confused monads having a certain range of points of view. What I perceive as a motion of my arm is a change in the points of view of all these monads. Now the change in the point of view of each of the arm-monads must in fact be caused by some previous change in it. The process d of deliberation in my mind corresponds to contemporary change δ_1, δ_2, ... in each of the subordinate monads m_1, m_2, ... of my organism. The change δ_1 in m_1 causes its point of view to change from π_1 to π_1'; the change δ_2 in m_2 causes its point of view to change from π_2 to π_2'; and so on for the rest. Meanwhile the process d in my mind causes my perception of them as my arm at position p to change to my perception of them as my arm at position p'. Thus, *in my mind* the conative process d leads by purely immanent causation to this change in my perceptions.

In the *arm-monads* the corresponding simultaneous processes δ_1, δ_2, ... lead to the changes in their points of view which I perceive. And by the Pre-established Harmony δ_1, δ_2, ... correspond to d; and the changes $\pi_1 \rightarrow \pi_1'$, $\pi_2 \rightarrow \pi_2'$, etc.,[1] correspond to the change from my perceiving the monads as my arm at position p to my perceiving them as my arm at position p'. The opposite case of a pin-prick seeming to produce a painful sensation would be dealt with in a similar way.

Sometimes we say that a person is 'active' in a certain transaction, e.g. when a man throws a stone. Sometimes we say that he is passive, e.g. when a stone hits a man and hurts him. Leibniz has to give an account of the facts underlying such statements which shall be consistent with his view that in neither case is there any interaction between one substance and another. His solution is as follows. Suppose that a stone hits me and that this event is immediately followed by my having a painful sensation. The occurrence of that sensation at that time must be wholly due to something in the previous state of my own mind. But I certainly cannot detect this past event in my mind either by introspection or retrospection. Therefore it must have been a very confused perception in me. Leibniz suggests that I am said to be 'passive' in any change when a distinct and noticeable change in my mind is caused by some factor in its previous state which was too faint or confused for me to be able to detect and discriminate by memory or introspection. Suppose, on the other hand, that I deliberately throw a stone. All that I really accomplish by my voluntary effort is to produce a change in my own perceptions; the changes in the monads which I perceive as the stone are caused by their own past states. But in this

[1] [I.e. the changes from π_1 to π_1', from π_2 to π_2', etc.]

case the cause of the change in my own perceptions is something which I can introspect and discriminate, viz. my voluntary effort. In such cases I am said to be 'active'.

The following quotations will make Leibniz's position clear. 'At the moment when the soul wills a bodily movement the organized mass which it animates is ready to act accordingly of itself in notice of the laws of mechanics' (*Système nouveau*).[1] 'Body and soul are so adapted that a resolution in the soul is accompanied by an appropriate movement in the body. . . Everything that goes on in the body is as if Hobbes and the Epicureans were right in holding that the soul is material or that there is no soul and a man is merely an automatic machine.' But philosophical considerations, such as the arguments about endless divisibility, the arguments from the nature of force in mechanics, the Predicate-in-Notion Principle, the denial of causal interaction, etc., show that materialism is neither adequate nor defensible if taken literally as a complete philosophical theory (*Second Answer to Bayle*).[2] 'The tendencies of the soul towards new *thoughts* correspond to the tendencies of the body towards new *shapes and motions*. As these new motions are capable of causing the body to pass from *order to disorder*, so their representations in the soul are capable of causing it to pass from *pleasure to pain*' (*Comments on the article Rorarius*).[3] 'Whatever happens in the body in accordance with the laws of mechanics is expressed in the soul according to its own laws' (*Letters to de Volder*).[4]

10 The Vinculum Substantiale

Before leaving Leibniz's theory of monads we must say something about a suggestion which he throws out in the *Letters to des Bosses* (1706–16). In estimating the weight to be attached to this suggestion it is important to remember the context in which Leibniz put it forward. Des Bosses was a Jesuit theologian, and Leibniz was anxious to show that the theory of monads could be reconciled with the Roman Catholic doctrine of transubstantiation. It is in this connexion that Leibniz puts forward the theory of the *Vinculum Substantiale*. So far as I can see, he never says that he himself holds this theory. He says that it would be consistent with the theory of monads and that it would give the Roman Catholics all that they could possibly demand in connexion with transubstantiation. It appears to me that Leibniz himself holds that the theory that ostensibly material things are *phenomena*

[1] [G., IV, 484. Loemker, 458.]   [2] [G., IV, 559. Loemker, 577.]
[3] [G., IV, 545.]   [4] [G., II, 205–6.]

bene fundata gives all that the Roman Catholics *ought* to demand.

It will be well to begin by stating the Roman Catholic doctrine of transubstantiation. So far as I can understand it, it is as follows. When the priest consecrates the bread and wine both the stuff and the form of those substances are abolished and they are replaced respectively by the stuff and the form of the body and the blood of Christ. But both the sensible and the dispositional properties of the bread and the wine continue to exist. E.g. the colour and smell of the wine and its chemical and physical properties remain. It is not a mere delusive appearance, but a fact independent of the observer, that these qualities and dispositional properties are still locally present. But, on the other hand, these accidents exist, after the consecration, in a quite peculiar way through the miraculous action of God. They no longer qualify any substance. St Thomas holds that the region formerly occupied by the bread and wine receives from God the power to act as the quasi-subject of the qualities and dispositions which formerly inhered in the substance of the bread and the wine.

Now Leibniz gives the following account of transubstantiation in terms of his own theory that what we perceive as a body is in fact an aggregate of unextended mental substances. Suppose that a certain aggregate of monads appears as a red body. Consider the scientific statement that the appearance of redness in ordinary light depends upon a certain kind of minute structure s in the surface of the body. Really the aggregate of monads which appears as a red body no more has this minute structure s than it has a red colour. For it is not really extended, and so it has no spatial structure. Yet in some sense the scientific statement is true. Leibniz's solution is as follows. We *consciously* perceive this aggregate of monads as a red body, and at the same time we *unconsciously* perceive it as having the minute structure s. Both this conscious perception and these unconscious perceptions are in part delusive. But it is a fact that our conscious misperception of this aggregate of monads as a *red* body depends causally upon our unconscious misperceptions of it as a body having the *minute structure s*. If we unconsciously misperceived a certain aggregate of monads as a body with a certain other minute structure s' we should consciously misperceive it as a *blue* body. And so on. Consider now the statement 'God has made this red body blue, but has preserved the accident of redness.' The phenomenalist interpretation of this would be as follows. 'God has so changed this aggregate of monads that anyone who perceives it will unconsciously misperceive it as a body with the minute structure s' instead of a body with the minute structure s. But he has miraculously arranged that everyone shall continue consciously to misperceive it as *red*, although normally an aggregate which is unconsciously misperceived as a body of the structure *s'* is consciously misperceived as a *blue* body.' Now apply this to the bread which has been consecrated. The monads are so changed that everyone unconsciously misperceives them in the way which would normally give rise to a conscious misperception of them as a lump of Christ's flesh. But, owing to God's further miraculous intervention, we all continue to misperceive them consciously as a wafer of bread.

Now this solution was not satisfactory to the Roman Catholics. They wanted something less phenomenalistic. It was in order to meet this requirement and yet keep the theory of monads that Leibniz threw out the suggestion of the *Vinculum Substantiale*.

I do not pretend to understand the doctrine of the *Vinculum Substantiale* in detail, but the following is pretty certainly a correct account, so far as it goes, of Leibniz's various statements.

(1) Leibniz's normal view, apart from the *Vinculum Substantiale* theory, is that the only genuine *substances* are *simple* substances, i.e. monads. There are no such things as composite substances. There are aggregates of simple substances, and we perceive some of these as bodies, i.e. as composite substances; but this is a misperception. He even goes further than this in the letter to des Bosses of 29 May 1716. He says there that an aggregate is a mere phenomenon. And he gives as his reason that everything in it except the monads is added by the mind of the percipient who perceives them together.[1] I think that this is a more extreme view than he generally takes. I think that he usually talks as if an organism really were an aggregate of monads, interrelated in a certain characteristic way, and as if our misperception consisted only in perceiving such an aggregate as a body. But, if we take the denial of relations seriously, we should no doubt be forced to the more extreme view that there are no genuine aggregates.

(2) The *Vinculum Substantiale* theory is intended to allow for the existence of genuine composite substances, independent of an observer and his perceptions. He says repeatedly that the *Vinculum Substantiale* is something which 'reifies' or 'substantializes' phenomena; which 'allows us to assign reality to phenomena outside perception'. Whether there is a *Vinculum Substantiale* or not, certain aggregates of monads *appear to us* as extended, massive, movable, composite substances. If there is no *Vinculum Substantiale*, they *only* appear to be such to minds like ours. If there is a *Vinculum Substantiale*, there is something con-

[1] [G., II, 517.]

nected with such an aggregate of monads, which *really* is extended, massive, movable, etc., whether we perceive it or not.

(3) Leibniz says that the only ostensibly corporeal substances in connexion with which it is plausible to postulate a *Vinculum Substantiale* are the bodies of living men or animals. In terms of his general theory of organisms this implies that it is only where you have a dominant monad and an organism of subordinate monads that it is plausible to suppose that there is a *Vinculum Substantiale*, which combines these subordinate monads into a genuine corporeal substance independent of the observer and his perceptions. How he reconciles this with his application of the theory to the bread and wine in the eucharist I do not understand.

(4) He says that the *Vinculum Substantiale* unifies the *materiae primae* of the various monads in an organism, and thus gives rise to the *materia prima* of a living body. It also unifies the entelechies of the various monads, and thus gives rise to the entelechy of that living body. This entelechy must be distinguished from the soul of the man or animal. The soul is the dominant monad, and is a simple immaterial substance. The entelechy of the body, which arises from the unification by the *Vinculum Substantiale* of the entelechies of the various monads in the organism, is in perpetual flux. For monads are constantly entering and leaving the organism. The soul or dominant monad, and the entelechy of the body which that soul animates, together constitute the *substantial form* of the individual man or animal.

(5) Leibniz, as we know, held that every living organism is, in a sense, ingenerable and incorruptible in the ordinary course of nature. For every organism is animated by a soul; every soul exists throughout the whole course of history and at every moment animates an organism; and, although the organism animated by a soul is never identical in content at any two moments, yet there is never complete discontinuity in its content even at crises such as conception and death. He concluded from this that, if there is a *Vinculum Substantiale* which unifies the monads in an organism, it too must be ingenerable and incorruptible in the ordinary course of nature.

(6) Leibniz makes the following statements about the relation between a *Vinculum Substantiale* and the monads which it unifies. (a) He insists that, when a set of monads is unified by a *Vinculum Substantiale* into a genuine composite substance, the monads are not *ingredients* in the *Vinculum* or in the composite substance thus formed. The monads are physically, but not metaphysically, requisite to the *Vinculum Substantiale* which unifies them. It could exist without unifying them, and

they could exist without being unified by it. (b) He means something much more radical by this than the tame proposition that the same *Vinculum Substantiale* need not unify precisely the same monads at all moments. In his letter to des Bosses of 29 May 1716 he says that a *Vinculum Substantiale* is 'naturally, but not essentially' a unifier of monads.[1] It can exist without unifying monads. In the ordinary course of nature God does not create a *Vinculum Substantiale* apart from a set of monads for it to unify; but there is no logical or metaphysical necessity for it to be actually unifying a set of monads. In the letter of 20 September 1712 he says that a *Vinculum Substantiale* which has been unifying certain monads can be transferred by God to others, thus unifying the latter with a genuine composite substance and leaving the former ununified and only apparently a substance.[2] Another possibility is that a certain *Vinculum Substantiale*, which already unifies a certain set of monads in the ordinary course of nature, may continue to do so but may also begin miraculously to unify a certain other set of monads. (c) When a composite substance is constituted out of an aggregate of monads by means of a *Vinculum Substantiale*, the *Vinculum* is neither a modification of these monads severally nor a relation between them collectively. Conversely, the monads which are unified by a *Vinculum Substantiale* are not accidents of that *Vinculum*. But it is an accident of the *Vinculum* that it unifies those particular monads at that moment (letter of 5 February 1712).[3] (d) All the modifications which occur *naturally* in a composite substance result from the modifications in the monads which are unified by a *Vinculum Substantiale* to form that substance. But God can by a miracle give to a *Vinculum Substantiale*, and to the composite substance which it produces, certain modifications which do not arise from and correspond to modifications in the monads. He can also miraculously deprive a *Vinculum Substantiale*, and the composite substances which it generates, of certain modifications which would naturally arise from the modifications of the monads (letter of 29 April 1715).[4]

These are the main points in Leibniz's doctrine of the *Vinculum Substantiale*. So far as I can understand, the application to the doctrine of transubstantiation is as follows. Before the priest has consecrated the bread it is a genuine substance consisting of a certain aggregate of monads unified by a certain *Vinculum Substantiale*. (I do not see how

[1] [G., II, 516.]
[2] [G., II, 458. Loemker, 606.]
[3] [G., II, 435–6. Loemker, 600–1.]
[4] [G., II, 495–6. Loemker, 610–11.]

this can be reconciled with his statement that only living organisms are genuine composite substances.) At the moment of consecration this *Vinculum Substantiale* is miraculously destroyed, and the *Vinculum* which unifies the monads of Christ's body is substituted for it. But the monads, which were formerly unified by the *Vinculum* which has now been destroyed, remain otherwise unchanged. So we continue to perceive them, both consciously and unconsciously, as a corporeal substance having all the characteristic sensible and structural and dispositional properties of a bit of bread.

So much for the doctrine of the *Vinculum Substantiale*. I have tried to state it as clearly as I can; but I must confess that the various statements call up no clear positive idea in *my* mind of what Leibniz may have had in *his* mind.

5

PSYCHOLOGY AND THEORY OF KNOWLEDGE

Leibniz brings out his own views on the nature of the mind and its activities largely in the course of criticizing Descartes and Locke.[1] Probably his most important and characteristic psychological doctrine is his assertion that there are 'unconscious perceptions' and his distinction between 'perception' and 'apperception'. He based his criticism of Locke and Descartes and his own positive psychological theories very largely on this. So we will begin with it.

1 Conscious and unconscious experiences

Leibniz used the word 'perception' in a very wide sense. It will do no harm if for the present we substitute the word 'experience' for it. Instances of experiences are feeling toothache, feeling frightened of a snake, feeling a desire for one's dinner, seeing a chair, ostensibly seeing a ghost, dreaming of falling off a roof, and so on.

1.1 Are unconscious experiences possible?

Now I think that the question about the possibility and the actuality of unconscious experiences may best be approached as follows. Sometimes, if you ask a person whether he is having an experience of a certain kind which you describe, he will answer 'Yes' without any preliminary effort of introspective attention and with complete conviction. That would be the case, e.g., if you were to ask me: 'Are you now seeing a bit of paper with writing in your own hand upon it?' Sometimes, if you put a similar question to a person, he will answer 'No' without any preliminary effort of introspective attention and with complete conviction. That would be the case, e.g., if you were now to ask me: 'Are you now hearing a bugle-call?' Sometimes a person hesitates about saying 'Yes' or 'No', and returns a qualified answer;

[1] [See especially the *New Essays*, Preface and Books I and II. G., V, 39–250. Langley, 41–284.]

but some such hesitations and qualifications are irrelevant to the question of unconscious experiences. E.g. you might say to a person: 'Do you see a man over there?' and he might hesitate to say either 'Yes' or 'No' because he was not sure whether what he saw was a man or a scarecrow. He might still say without hesitation: 'I see something that looks like a man, but I may be mistaken in thinking it to be a man.' Again, suppose that a person were in a feverish state with periods of delirium and periods of normal consciousness, and that he was aware of the fact. If you said to him: 'Do you see a man over there?', he might hesitate to say 'Yes' or 'No', simply because he was not sure whether the word 'see' is appropriate to describe his visual or quasi-visual experience. He might still say without hesitation: 'I seem to see a man, but this may be an hallucinatory visual experience, and I may not really be *seeing* a man or any other physical object.'

Now there are other cases where a person, when asked such a question, would hesitate and begin to perform a process of introspective attention before attempting to say 'Yes' or 'No'. Suppose I were sitting in a room with another person and he suddenly said to me: 'Do you smell gas?' I should probably not be prepared to answer either 'Yes' or 'No' offhand. If I knew him to be a normal sensible person I should assume that there was a motive for his question and that he at any rate was having an olfactory experience which suggested to him that there was an escape of gas. I might have been attending to other matters, and I should now start sniffing and attending specially to my sensations of smell. After doing so I might either say 'Yes' with conviction or 'No' with conviction or 'I am not quite sure whether I do or do not.' And here the doubt would be, not as to whether an experience of smell which I certainly have is really due to the presence of gas, but as to whether I am or am not having an experience which might be described as 'smelling a gas-like smell'. Suppose that, when I do start sniffing and specially attending to my sensations of smell, I am able to say without hesitation: 'Yes, I am smelling a gas-like smell', this does not in itself settle the question whether I *was* having such an experience at the time when the question was asked, i.e. just *before* I began to sniff and to attend selectively. It is obviously possible that these processes may have been necessary conditions for producing in me an experience which I was not having before.

I think that the question of the possibility of unconscious experiences may now be put as follows. Is it *intelligible* to say of a person: '*C* is having an experience of such-and-such a kind at the moment *t*', if all the following conditions are fulfilled? (1) The phrase 'having an experience of such-and-such a kind' is used in precisely the same sense in which it is used when a person who is asked whether he is having an experience of that kind unhesitatingly answers 'Yes'. (2) If the question had been put to X at t and he had answered honestly, he would either (a) have at once unhesitatingly answered 'No', or (b) could have unhesitatingly answered 'No' if he had then started a process of introspective attention directed towards settling the question. As this is rather abstract, I will take a concrete example. Is it intelligible to say 'Mr Jones is now having a sensory or quasi-sensory experience of a ticking noise' if all the following conditions are fulfilled? (1) The phrase is used in precisely the same sense in which it is used when one says to a person: 'Are you aware of a ticking noise?' and he unhesitatingly answers 'Yes', even though he may admit that the experience may be hallucinatory or an auditory illusion. (2) If the question were put to Mr Jones now and he were to answer honestly, he would either (a) unhesitatingly answer 'No', at once, or (b) would do so at the end of a process of introspective attention devoted to settling the question. If and only if it is intelligible, when all these conditions are fulfilled, to say that Mr Jones is having a sensory or quasi-sensory experience of a ticking noise, it is intelligible to say that Mr Jones is having an *unconscious* perception or quasi-perception of a ticking noise, in a perfectly literal non-dispositional sense. There may be, and no doubt are, other senses of the phrase 'unconscious experiences' in which to say that a person is having an unconscious experience of such-and-such a kind would merely be saying something about his dispositions, i.e. about what experiences he *would* have or *would* have had, if certain conditions should be or had been fulfilled. These may be called 'metaphorical and dispositional' senses of the phrase 'unconscious experiences'. I think there is no doubt that Leibniz held it to be intelligible to say that a person may have unconscious experiences in the literal non-dispositional sense which I have explained. And there is no doubt that he held that this possibility is in fact realized, and that every person does have unconscious experiences in the literal non-dispositional sense.

If a man alleges that it is unintelligible to say that there may be unconscious experiences in the literal non-dispositional sense, he must, I think, accept the following two propositions. (1) That it is part of what we mean by calling an event an 'experience' that we could say of it: 'Some one person X has that experience.' (2) That it is part of what we mean by saying that X has the experience e that, if e were described to X at the time when it is occurring, X could, if asked whether he was having it, answer, either at once or after a process of introspective attention, with complete confidence that he was. I suppose that Leibniz would have accepted the first and rejected the second of these two propositions. He would not have thought it intelligible to say that there might be experiences which were not the experiences of anyone. But he did think it intelligible to say that a person might be having an experience of a certain kind, although, if you had asked him at the time whether he was doing so and he had answered honestly, he would have answered, either at once or after a process of introspective attention, with complete confidence in the negative.

So far as I am aware Leibniz assumes this without any discussion, and concerns himself simply with arguments to prove that the assumed possibility of unconscious experiences is in fact realized.

1.2 Leibniz's arguments for unconscious experiences

I shall not go into Leibniz's empirical arguments in detail, because I have discussed such arguments pretty fully in *The Mind and its Place in Nature* (Chapter 9).[1] But there are some general remarks which it may be worth while to make about them.

If we look into these arguments, I think we find that they all rest on one or other of the following three tacit assumptions. (1) If I perceive a whole which in fact has several parts or several characteristics, then I must *ipso facto* perceive all the parts and all the characteristics of that perceived whole. (2) If the physical stimulus which gives rise to a perception is complex, then every part of that complex stimulus must give rise to a different perception. Leibniz evidently uses this as a premiss in his favourite argument that our hearing of the roaring of the sea at a distance must be composed of innumerable unconscious auditory perceptions of each wave rolling on each stone. Our conscious perception of the noise of the surf on the shore is composed of, or built upon, our unconscious perceptions of the noises due to the rolling of each wave on each stone. (3) What is called the 'persistent innate or acquired power' to cognize a certain object *x* is really the process of cognizing *x* continually. What is called 'stimulating the disposition into action' is really the raising of this continuous cognitive process from the unconscious to the conscious level from time to time.

(1) As regards the first of these premisses it is perhaps plausible about *parts*, but it is not so as regards *characteristics*. It is plausible to say that, if

[1] [C. D. Broad, *The Mind and Its Place in Nature* (London, 1925).]

I literally see the whole of the top surface of a penny, then there must be a sense in which I literally see every part of that surface. It is surely not plausible to say that I must perceive all its qualities.

(2) I do not think that Leibniz has any right to use the second premiss, and, even if he had, it is not particularly plausible. It is plain that he ought not to use, without some kind of elaborate reinterpretation in terms of his own theory of monads, a premiss which presupposes the commonsense view that our sensations are occasioned by the action of foreign bodies on our own bodies. For he has rejected the reality both of matter and of transeunt causation.

(3) The third premiss needs some further discussion. It is plain that some of the empirical arguments which Leibniz uses to prove the existence of unconscious *perceptions* would directly prove only the existence of certain *cognitive dispositions*. Now these are not perceptions or any other kind of actual experiences. Many philosophers, e.g. Descartes and Locke, who reject the notion of unconscious experiences as meaningless, have no objection to cognitive dispositions. I suspect that Leibniz may have argued as follows.

Suppose, e.g., that I have learned something and can actually remember it when I choose to or when I am suitably reminded. At other times I am certainly not consciously thinking of it, and there seems *prima facie* no need to postulate anything relevant to it in my mind during these intervals except a certain persistent cognitive disposition. But, after all, a disposition is merely a disguised conditional proposition. Most of us feel obliged to suppose that there is some actual state or modification which was set up by the original process of learning, which persists thereafter, and which cooperates with any subsequent reminder to produce an actual experience of remembering. But how is this persistent state or modification to be conceived? Many people would think of it as a structural modification in the brain or nervous system. But Leibniz could not take that view. For according to him what is called the 'brain' is really a set of confused monads partly misperceived, and none of these can act on the mind, which is the dominant monad of this set. So the persistent modification must for him be something purely mental. Now it is not at all easy to conceive of a persistent mental modification, since it cannot be thought of as a modification in spatial arrangement or motion of particles. It seems to me that the view which Leibniz took was that the modification simply is a persistent but unconscious experience. E.g. during intervals when I should ordinarily be said not to be thinking of the fact that $2 \times 2 = 4$ and not to be remembering the late Master of

Trinity, I am really continuously thinking of the former and remembering the latter in a perfectly literal non-dispositional sense. But at such times these experiences are unconscious. At times when it would ordinarily be said that the mere cognitive disposition gives rise to an actual experience what really happens is that the cognitive process which has been going on all the time becomes *conscious*. Thus for Leibniz any evidence for cognitive *dispositions* would *ipso facto* be evidence for unconscious cognitive *experiences*.

1.3 'Minute' and 'confused' perceptions

Leibniz has a great deal to say about what he calls 'minute perceptions' and what he calls 'confused perceptions'; and he thinks that there is a close connexion between minuteness and confusion, on the one hand, and unconscious perception, on the other.

By a 'minute perception' he meant one of very faint intensity. He does not distinguish very sharply between act and object in the case of sensations. But it is evident that a sensation of a very faint or very inextensive sensibile would *ipso facto* be a perception of very faint intensity. Thus the sensation of a just audible squeak, or of a colour expanse so small as to be only just visible, would be a minute perception. Now Leibniz thought that minuteness tends to make a perception unconscious, and that if it be feeble enough it will inevitably be unconscious under normal conditions.

We come now to the notion of 'confusion'. Leibniz distinguishes carefully between 'confusion' and 'obscurity'. The opposite of confusion is *distinctness*, and the opposite of obscurity is *clearness*. He defines these terms explicitly with reference to ideas of species, but I think that his definition can be applied without much difficulty to perceptions of particulars.

You have a *clear* idea of a species, e.g. of sheep, if it would enable you to recognize an instance if you were to perceive one under normal conditions. If it would not enable you to do this, the idea is *obscure*. Now, when you have a clear idea of a species, and are thus enabled to recognize an instance of it, this must in fact be due to a certain set of characteristics which taken together are common and peculiar to members of the species. But you may not have analysed this set into its components and discriminated them. If you have done so your idea is *distinct* as well as clear. If you have not, it is *confused*, though clear. Thus the ordinary person has a clear idea of the species man; but, in so far as the feature by which he recognizes that something is a man is a highly complex and unanalysed shape, size, posture, colour, etc., the idea is confused. An anatomist or physiologist would have a much *more distinct*, though not necessarily a *clearer*, idea of man.

Let us now apply this to the perception of a particular. Anything that we perceive will have many characteristics and it may have many parts. Some of these characteristics and some of these parts may be discriminated by the percipient and others may not. The perception of an object is said to be 'confused' when the object has in fact parts or characteristics which the percipient does not discriminate. As I have said, Leibniz seems to have regarded it as axiomatic that, if I am acquainted with a whole W, which in fact consists of the parts P_1, P_2, . . . and which in fact has the characteristics C_1, C_2, . . ., then I must *ipso facto* be acquainted with all these parts and all these characteristics. If I fail to discriminate some of these parts or characteristics, that can mean only that my perceptions of them are unconscious. They may be unconscious either because of their minuteness or because they are all extremely alike and are all happening at the same time. Of course both these causes may cooperate to make them unconscious.

Thus the connexion between unconsciousness, minuteness, and confusion may be summarized as follows. A perception tends to be unconscious if either (a) its immediate object is very feeble in intensity or very inextensive, or (b) it is one of a number of very similar perceptions which are all happening at the same time in the same mind. A confused perception is a perception of an object which has certain parts or certain characteristics which the percipient does not *consciously* perceive. Since he must be perceiving them all, he must be perceiving *unconsciously* those which he does not perceive consciously. And the perceptions of these parts or characteristics will be unconscious either because of their minuteness or because of their likeness to each other or for both reasons.

1.4 Leibniz's uses of the doctrine of unconscious experiences

We come now to the uses which Leibniz made of the doctrine of unconscious experiences in his own philosophy. The doctrine was absolutely essential for some purposes and very useful for others. Leibniz enumerates them in the *New Essays*. (1) If the Pre-established Harmony is to be a substitute for the generalized physical principle that everything acts on everything else, we must suppose that every monad perceives every other monad. Now it is certain that I do not consciously perceive everything else in the universe. Therefore it is only by admitting that I perceive a great deal unconsciously that it could be admitted that I perceive everything else in the universe. (2) By means of unconscious experiences we can explain how it seems that some of our choices are not completely determined, although really they are completely determined. (3) There is plainly more in a self than its conscious sensations, and thoughts, and memories at any moment. The latter are very fragmentary and superficial. The background and foundation of personality is unconscious, minute, and confused perceptions. (4) The doctrine of unconscious mental states explains how death can be merely a sleep, and how the soul can have existed before birth. (5) It enables us to explain the relations between primary and secondary qualities in a more satisfactory way than Descartes and Locke had been able to do. (6) It explains how desire can move us to action and yet often be a pleasant rather than a painful experience. I will explain the last two statements later.

1.4.1 Is a mind always thinking?

We can now explain how Leibniz used his doctrine of unconscious perceptions in connexion with two controversies between Locke and Descartes. Descartes held that the mind must always think, i.e. always be performing some actual cognitive process. Locke said that there was no reason why it must, and that in all probability it does not during dreamless sleep. Again Descartes accepted innate ideas and innate principles whilst Locke rejected both. The position which Leibniz takes is this. It is common ground to Locke and Descartes that a person cannot have an experience without *ipso facto* knowing simultaneously that he has it. On this common basis Locke's arguments against Descartes are conclusive. And yet Descartes was in fact right in holding that the mind must think always and that there are innate ideas and principles. What is needed is to distinguish between conscious and unconscious experiences and to admit that a person can have experiences which he is not automatically aware of having at the time. In that case it can be maintained that the mind cognizes even during periods of dreamless sleep. For we have only to suppose that it cannot now, and perhaps did not then, cognize its own cognitive acts which it performed during sleep. It is clear that, if we accept this doctrine of Leibniz's all Locke's arguments against the principle that the mind is always actually cognizing fall to the ground. But is there any positive ground for accepting the principle? According to Leibniz there is.

In the first place, he accepts Descartes's premiss that cognition is the essential attribute of the mind, and merely insists against Descartes that cognition need not be conscious. He agrees with Descartes that the fact that cognition is the essential attribute entails that the mind must be continually cognizing. But, apart from this, he has, on his own premisses, perfectly conclusive empirical arguments. For everyone must admit that during dreamless sleep, fainting, etc., the mind must have persistent cognitive *dispositions*. Otherwise the linking up of this morning's experiences with last night's would be inexplicable. And, as we have seen, Leibniz holds that what is called a persistent cognitive *disposition* must really be a continuous non-introspectible cognitive *process*.

2 The innate and the a priori

Leibniz's theory of innate and *a priori* principles and concepts needs separate discussion. Of course his doctrine of unconscious cognition enables him at once to answer all the objections to innate concepts and beliefs which Locke based on babies, idiots, and savages. We are at all times thinking of and believing the laws of logic, arithmetic, etc. But at most times in all of us and at all times in some of us this cognition remains unnoticed and undiscriminated. It may nevertheless affect our action and our conscious thinking, so that we tend to obey these principles and feel uncomfortable when we disobey them, even when we do not explicitly recognize them. It may need a great deal of attention, and even special instruction, to enable us to become aware of our knowledge of these principles; and it is quite likely that children and savages whose interests are mainly practical will not take the trouble to do this.

Leibniz admits that, on his view, all ideas are in a certain sense innate. This seems to me to be the case both in a negative and in a positive sense. The negative sense is that none of my ideas can have been put into me by the action of anything outside my mind. If they have originated at all in the course of my history they must have been completely caused by earlier events in my mind. This, however, would still make it possible to draw a distinction between ideas and beliefs which had always existed in my mind, consciously or unconsciously, and others which did not exist even unconsciously in my mind until a certain date in my history. The former might be called innate in the positive sense; the latter would be innate only in the negative sense of internally generated. But, when we remember Leibniz's view of change, I think we shall have to say that all my ideas and beliefs are innate in the positive sense. For he holds that the only changes are changes in the distribution of confusion and distinctness over the same field of consciousness. If so, God created me with all the ideas that I shall ever have; and all that has happened since is that some have become conscious whilst others have become unconscious. How this doctrine could be reconciled with the fact that I sometimes change my opinion about the same subject, e.g. start by believing p, go on to doubt it, and end up by disbelieving it, I do not know.

The distinction between innate and acquired thus ceases to be very important for Leibniz. But he says that he can use the distinction in a certain special sense, and that in this sense it is important. He can distinguish between those concepts which are derived by abstraction from sense-perception, or which are constructed from concepts thus derived, and those which are not. That is, he can distinguish between what I should call 'empirical' and '*a priori*' concepts as well as anyone else. Again, he can distinguish between those universal judgments which are merely empirical generalizations, and those which can be seen to be necessary. That is, he can distinguish between what I should call 'empirical' and '*a priori*' judgments as well as anyone else.

Now among *a priori* concepts, in the sense defined, he counts the concepts of God, of the self, of substance, cause, and the other categories. And he holds a rather special view of the way in which we acquire explicit ideas of the categories. We acquire them by reflecting on ourselves as agents, substances, etc. I think his position may be summed up as follows. The concepts of God, the self, and the categories, are, like all concepts, innate. All that is needed is to make conscious the unconscious ideas of them, which we all have. They are *a priori* in the sense that they are not made explicit by a process of abstraction from sense-experiences. But some special kind of experience is needed to start the process which will render them explicit. And in the case of the categories of cause, substance, etc., there is nothing in our sense-experiences to start the process. What starts it is reflexion on ourselves as active agents and as the unitary owners of a series of infinitely complex total states. The concepts of pure geometry are equally innate and equally *a priori*. But there the special kind of experience which is needed to start the process of making them conscious and explicit does come from sense-perception, though the process is not one of mere abstraction from sense-experience. Leibniz objects to Locke's comparison of the mind to a *tabula rasa*. He says that it is more like a block of white marble with black veins in it which mark out a statue. We have only to chip away the white surroundings and the statue will stand out. I think he means by this that, among its other ideas, every rational soul contains the idea of itself as a nucleus, and that reflexion on itself and its nature suffices to make explicit the categories of cause, substance, etc.

3 Sensation and sense-perception

Leibniz's views on sensation and sense-perception are not very easy to make out. It is certain that he held that sensation is highly confused, that it is by means of sensation that we learn of the existence and qualities of substances other than ourselves, and that we are in some way passive in sensation as compared with thinking. Kant often accuses Leibniz of holding that sensation is merely confused thought, and he rightly insists that such a doctrine is quite impossible. But I very much doubt whether Leibniz ever held it in the sense in which Kant denied it. If we contrast sensation, as *intuitive* acquaintance with particulars, and *thought*, as discursive cognition by means of judgments about the qualities and relations of subjects, it seems to me most unlikely that Leibniz ever held that sensation is confused thought. We must now try to make out what he may have meant.

3.1 Primary and secondary qualities

(1) In the first place, he distinguishes between the sensible qualities which we sense by the special senses, e.g. colour, temperature, etc., and those which we become acquainted with by what he calls 'the *common sense*'. Among the latter are included all such qualities as shape, size, number, duration, etc., which Locke held to be derived from several senses, such as sight and touch, or from both sensation and reflexion. Leibniz places our ideas of these latter qualities on a higher intellectual level than our ideas of the former. His reason seems to be that the latter give rise to the *a priori* concepts and judgments of pure geometry, whilst no *a priori* concepts or judgments are suggested by the special sensations of colour, temperature, smell, etc. (2) He says that the ideas which come from the special senses are clear but not distinct. The idea of red, e.g., is a clear idea; for we have no difficulty in recognizing a red thing when we see it. But it is not distinct for the following reason. If we accept the orthodox physical view, what is perceived as red is certain vibrations which have in fact no colour but have a certain vibration-number. Leibniz, when talking as a physicist, seems to hold

that to perceive something as red simply is to perceive confusedly a large number of very similar disturbances in a very short period. The whole is perceived confusedly because each disturbance is so minute and lasts for so short a time; and because they are all so much alike. Consequently, though each is perceived, the perception of each is unconscious. And so the perception of the whole composed of them is confused. I suppose that the ordinary view is that we do not perceive the vibrations at all, but that they produce an effect in us which is a sensation of a red colour-expanse. Leibniz's view, at the level at which we are at present moving, seems to be that we actually perceive the vibrations and not an effect of them; and that we misperceive a set of similar vibrations, which all occur in a very short period, as red, because our perception of each is unconscious and so our perception of the whole set is confused. Of course this cannot be his ultimate view; for, according to him there are really no vibrations and no extended surfaces. But his theory of our perception of extended surfaces is similar. What I actually perceive is a set of very numerous and very similar monads. Owing to their number and their likeness my perception of each of them is unconscious, and so my perception of the set as a whole is confused. And to perceive the set as extended just is to perceive it in this confused way. (3) Thus Leibniz can allow a relative, but only a relative, validity to Locke's distinction between primary and secondary qualities. The primary qualities are what we become acquainted with by the common sense. Our sensations of them stimulate us to become conscious of certain *a priori* concepts and judgments (viz. the concepts and axioms of pure geometry and mechanics) which make them susceptible of scientific treatment. The secondary qualities are what we become acquainted with by the special senses. They are correlated with certain primary qualities, and become capable of scientific treatment only through this correlation. At the half-scientific and half-philosophic level of Locke's *Essay* we can say that to perceive something as a red surface just is to perceive confusedly a set of vibrations of a certain frequency, and so on. But, when we speak with strict philosophical correctness, we must add that to perceive something as having extension and shape and motion is to perceive confusedly an infinitely numerous set of unextended monads of very similar points of view.

I think that we must here distinguish two alternative possible views, both about secondary qualities and about primary qualities. One view about our awareness of secondary qualities would be that a conscious perception of something as red just *consists* of a vast number of unconscious perceptions of vibrations of a certain frequency within a very short period. The other view would be that to have a vast number of unconscious perceptions of vibrations of a certain frequency within a very short period is a *causally necessary condition* for having a conscious perception of something as red, but that the latter conscious experience is *not composed of* the former unconscious experiences. Similarly one view about our perception of something as a surface of a certain shape and size would be that it is a conscious perception *composed of* a vast number of simultaneous unconscious perceptions of monads whose points of view are very much alike. The other view would be that to have a vast number of simultaneous unconscious perceptions of monads whose points of view are very much alike is a *causally necessary condition* for having a conscious perception of something as a surface of a certain shape and size, but that the latter conscious experience is *not composed of* the former unconscious experiences. On the first alternative, the property of being a conscious perception of something as red or being a conscious perception of something as extended and shaped would be a kind of collective or pattern-quality. That is to say, it would belong to a certain collection of simultaneous or closely successive perceptions taken as a whole. But it would not belong to any of them individually. None of them would be a *conscious* perception or a perception of anything as *red* or a perception of anything as *extended and shaped*. On the second alternative, the property of being a conscious perception of something as red or of something as extended and shaped would belong neither to the individual unconscious perceptions nor to the collection of them taken as a whole. It would belong to another perception, which arises as an effect of their simultaneous or closely successive occurrences. It seems to me that Leibniz ought to hold the second alternative. For to admit the possibility of collective or pattern-qualities would be to admit the possibility of attributes which have as many 'legs' as a centipede, and he has rejected relations on the ground that there could not be an attribute 'with one leg in one term and another leg in another term'.

3.2 Direct versus representative perception

There is one question which it is worth while to raise before leaving Leibniz's theory of sense-perception. Does his theory necessarily involve the doctrine of 'representative perception'? Or would it be compatible with his general principles that one monad should be directly acquainted with other monads?

I understand by the theory of representative perception the two following propositions. (1) The only objects with which a person can possibly be acquainted are internal objects, i.e. states of his own mind. (2) Some of these internal objects are specially related to certain things or events other than his own mind and its states, and in virtue of this are 'representative' to him of these foreign things and events. In being acquainted with such a representative internal object a person automatically but indirectly perceives the foreign thing or event which this internal object represents. I understand by the theory of direct perception that a person may be and sometimes is acquainted with a foreign thing or event.

Now it is commonly assumed that Leibniz held the theory of representative perception. I think that many people would be inclined to say that his statement that 'monads have no windows'[1] is conclusive evidence for this. I am inclined to agree that he did hold the theory, but I do not think that this quotation is conclusive. Windows can be considered from two different points of view, viz. as holes through which one can look out at the rest of the world, or as holes through which causal influences from the rest of the world may blow in. When Leibniz says that monads have no windows he is thinking of the latter analogy and not the former.

It seems to me that he could consistently have held that one monad is directly acquainted with other monads, though I do not suggest that he actually did hold this. In each monad a series of acts of acquaintance would arise from purely internal causes. But the immediate object of each such act would be another monad in the state which it had then reached in the course of its own internal development. On this view, when I am said to be perceiving a bit of matter, I am directly but unconsciously acquainted with every one of a certain very numerous set of monads, with very similar points of view, in the state which they have then reached. In some way, not satisfactorily explained, the coexistence of all these unconscious acts of acquaintance with these numerous individual monads either constitutes or causes in me a confused perception of the group as a whole. This is a misperception of that group as a single, continuously extended coloured massive material thing. That Leibniz did not in fact hold the theory of direct perception is, I think, clear from the fact that he says that the perceptions of each monad would have been unaltered even if all the others had been annihilated.

[1] [G., VI, 607. Loemker, 643.]

4 Conative and affective experiences

Conation is just as essential a feature of every monad as cognition. When the striving of a monad is accompanied and directed by a conscious belief that such-and-such a future state of affairs would satisfy it, it is called *desire*. When it is not thus accompanied and directed it is called *instinct*. In the case of desire the accompanying belief may be mistaken in detail or completely. Leibniz holds that in the actual world every monad strives for its own good. This is supposed to be a contingent fact. It is not very easy to see what it can mean. It is obvious that conscious beings often desire what will in fact be bad for them, owing to mistaken beliefs. So one would be tempted to substitute for Leibniz's contingent principle the principle that every monad strives for what it *believes at the time* to be its own good. But, even if this be admitted for self-conscious rational monads acting deliberately, it is difficult to see what it can mean for animal souls and bare monads, in which striving takes the form of instinct. Perhaps Leibniz would say that in instinctive action the striving is accompanied and directed by an *unconscious* belief that such-and-such a future state would be good for the agent.

Leibniz holds that pleasure and pain are indefinable, in the sense that no analysis can be given of the notion of pleasant and painful. But he thinks it is a true synthetic proposition that a perception is pleasant if and only if it noticeably helps our activity. Similarly a perception is painful if and only if it noticeably hinders our activity. It is probable that every perception has one or other of these effects to some degree; but when the effect is so slight as not to be noticed the experience is counted as hedonically neutral. He also expresses his belief that pleasure is a noticeable feeling of perfection and pain a noticeable feeling of imperfection. Now, like Spinoza, he always identifies increase of perfection with increase of cognitive distinctness and decrease of perfection with increase of cognitive confusion. So it looks as if his doctrine amounted to this, that pleasure is the sign of any change in us that makes us noticeably less confused, and that pain is the sign of any change in us that makes us noticeably more confused. He defines 'happiness' as lasting pleasure, and says that it can be realized only by continually passing from one pleasant experience to another. 'Happiness,' he says, 'is a road through pleasures.'[1] Reason shows us the best road. Instinct and passion try to take short-cuts, and thus often lead us astray.

[1] [G., V, 180. Langley, 201.]

Leibniz's view of the nature of the experience of desiring is as follows. It is not itself painful. But it is a confused state made up of a number of undiscriminated minute experiences, each of which would be painful if it were magnified and separately noticed. As we satisfy a desire these minute undiscriminated *quasi*-pains are replaced by minute undiscriminated *quasi*-pleasures. At the end of the process the latter are integrated into an appreciable pleasure. It is difficult to see why the coexistence of a number of minute *quasi*-pleasures should be an actually pleasant experience, when the coexistence of a number of minute *quasi*-pains is not an actually painful experience.

Leibniz, like most philosophers of his time, was a psychological hedonist. He held that the only ultimate motive is the desire for our own happiness. Now pleasure is a noticeable feeling of perfection, and presumably the degree of the pleasure is proportional to the degree of perfection; so one's own greatest happiness would be one's own greatest perfection throughout the whole of one's life here and hereafter. Thus a person who desired his own greatest happiness, and knew in what this really consisted, would desire his own greatest perfection, i.e. would desire the maximum clearness of perception throughout life. But, whilst everyone desires his own greatest happiness, most people do not recognize that their own greatest happiness consists in their own greatest perfection, or that this consists in maximum clearness of knowledge. So men can and do desire other things, but they always do so under the misapprehension that these other things will make them as happy as possible.

6

ETHICS

Leibniz was a universalistic ethical hedonist. That is he held that nothing is intrinsically good but happiness or intrinsically bad but unhappiness, and that the more happiness there is the better no matter whether it is in A or B or C. Now, as he was also an egoistic psychological hedonist, the question arises: 'How can it be my duty to promote the happiness of other people, since it is psychologically impossible for me to desire anything but my own happiness as an end?' The way in which Leibniz attempts to answer this question seems to be as follows. When I clearly understand what my own happiness consists in I see that it consists in being intellectually as clear and as little confused as possible. I shall therefore aim at making myself as completely a reasonable a being as possible, simply because I shall see that my greatest happiness consists in this. Of course my approach to this state will presumably be in some respects a self-accelerating process. The more reasonable I become the more clearly I shall see that my greatest happiness consists in being as completely reasonable as possible. And the more clearly I see that my greatest happiness consists in being as reasonable as possible the more intensely and single-mindedly I shall aim at making myself reasonable. So far his doctrine is intelligible enough. He then claims that the more reasonable I become the more I shall aim at increasing the general happiness. I cannot see that the last step is valid. If Leibniz had said: 'The more reasonable you become the more clearly you will see that the best way to make yourself happy is to aim at making other people happy', it would have followed that an enlightened psychological hedonist ought to aim at the general happiness as a means though not as an end. But he does not say this, and I do not see how he consistently could have said it. If my greatest happiness consists in clear rational knowledge, I ought, as an enlightened psychological hedonist, to aim at making others happy only in so far as I can see that this is the best way to increase and clarify my own knowledge. And I cannot see any reason to suppose that this always or often could be the best means to this end.

I have little doubt that Leibniz's real view is that when we really know what we are about we see that the greatest happiness of each of us is best secured by practising what are ordinarily counted as virtues and without regard to their effects on our own happiness. Of course, even if this be accepted, the motive for what is called 'virtuous action' remains purely egoistic. We perform virtuous acts, not because they are virtuous, but because they are seen to be the best means to our own happiness. Still, this is a considerably more elevated form of egoism than Locke's or Paley's. According to them virtue can be chosen only because there is an *external* payment in this world or the next for virtuous action. On Leibniz's view 'virtue is its own reward', in the sense that the performance of what are ordinarily called 'virtuous actions' is itself pleasant and the most intense kind of pleasure to a rational being. Yet it must be admitted that Leibniz has failed to show, that, e.g., the practice of benevolence is so pleasant in itself to the agent that a really enlightened egoistic psychological hedonist would always practise benevolence. And it seems most unlikely that this could be proved or that it is in fact true.

It will be noticed that on Leibniz's view all wrong-doing is due to intellectual confusion. I necessarily do what I think at the moment will give me most happiness on the whole; and, unless I make a mistake about what will make me most happy, this line of conduct is also the one which will produce the greatest happiness on the whole, and is therefore the right line of conduct. Leibniz does not allow for weakness or perversity of will, i.e. seeing the better and failing to pursue it or deliberately rejecting it for the worse. This view that all wrong-doing is completely explicable by intellectual mistakes about certain matters of fact has, of course, been held by many other important philosophers beside Leibniz. It seems to me to be plainly false. There is a desire to do what is believed to be right as such; but there are other desires, which conflict with it, and which may and do overcome it at times without first clouding the intellect. And the doctrine is peculiarly inconvenient for Leibniz, who believes in eternal punishment. For even the most enthusiastic supporter of eternal punishment might hesitate to think that it is just for a spirit to be tortured eternally because its intellect had been at certain times too confused to see clearly what kinds of action would be most conducive to its happiness.

7

THEOLOGY

It is plain that God plays a very important part in Leibniz's system. He wrote one large book – the *Theodicy* – especially to deal with Bayle's doctrine that revealed religion is not merely supplementary, but positively contrary, to human reason. But the *Theodicy* contains much beside this, e.g. a justification of God's character, and the exposition of Leibniz's optimism. We will begin by stating Leibniz's view of the nature of God and his relation to the monads.

1 God's nature and relations to the world

Leibniz developed his view of God in contrast to those of Descartes and Spinoza. His own special theory of the nature of finite substances at once introduced a sharp difference between his view of the nature of God and their views. If Leibniz is right, there are genuine finite substances which owe their origin to God; but, once created, they continue to exist and develop from the active force which God has given them. They do not need to be recreated from moment to moment, as Descartes held. They are not mere occurrents in God as continuant, as Spinoza held. And they genuinely act and change from their own resources, instead of being perpetually pushed and pulled about by God, as the Occasionalists held. Of course Leibniz would not have been prepared to say that they are now wholly independent of God. In the first place, God could at any moment annihilate any of them by a miracle. Secondly, they require the perpetual concurrence of God as a necessary background condition for their continued existence and development. In the *Discours*, Section 14, e.g., Leibniz says that God continually keeps each substance in existence by a kind of *emanation*, and that this may be compared to the way in which we produce our own thoughts.[1] I think that all orthodox theologians would insist upon this amount of continual dependence of created substances upon God. But this leaves them much less dependent than they would if the views of Descartes or Spinoza or the Occasionalists were true. Now this view makes the notion of creation fundamental in Leibniz's

[1] [G., IV, 439. Loemker, 311.]

system. For 'to create', when used literally, just means to bring into being a genuine new substance, which can then continue and develop on its own without further special interference from its creator. This is quite a different notion from that of producing a new occurrent in a pre-existing continuant. And it is quite different from bringing certain pre-existing continuants into more intimate and relatively stable mutual relations, so that a new complex continuant is formed which then persists. We do the former if we set up a ripple which continues in a pond of water. We do the latter when we build a bridge or an engine. But we cannot genuinely create a new simple continuant, and we cannot conceive what such a process as genuine creation would be. Now Leibniz's God has to be creative, because Leibniz's monads are genuine simple continuants, and because Leibniz held that the monads had a beginning and that God started them. There is no pretence that Spinoza's God is creative. And, when Descartes's doctrine that persistence in perpetual recreation is thought out, one sees that it amounts to the denial of genuine finite substances and therefore to the denial of genuine creation.

Now it might be argued that the fact that Leibniz's God has to be creative is a serious defect in his system as compared, e.g., with Spinoza's. We know what we mean by the occurrent–continuant relation, at any rate in the sense that we think we can produce plenty of instances of it within the universe. And Spinoza uses only this relation. But we certainly do not know, even in this sense, what we mean by the relation of creator and created substance; since there are no instances of it within the universe. And Leibniz has to make use of this relation. There are two things to be said about this contention. (1) It must be said for Leibniz and against Spinoza that Spinoza can make the occurrent–continuant relation adequate *only* by counting as occurrents certain things which *prima facie* are not occurrents in any known continuant, viz. finite minds. (2) It might be possible to keep this advantage of Leibniz over Spinoza and yet avoid the notion of creation altogether. For it might be possible to hold that the ultimate simple continuants of which the universe is composed never originated and will never end. In that case we might either have no God, or a God who is one supremely important simple continuant but not a creator of other simple continuants. We should then get a system something like McTaggart's. Leibniz of course thought that there were conclusive reasons against such a view, and we shall have to consider them when we deal with his arguments for the existence of God.

Closely connected with the property of creativeness which Leibniz assigned to God is another difference between him and Descartes and Spinoza. He agreed with Spinoza in rejecting Descartes's view that both the difference between right and wrong and the difference between truth and falsehood depend on the arbitrary decrees of God. But Spinoza, in rejecting this, also rejected the view that God contemplates genuine possibilities, weighs up the good and bad points in each, and then decides to actualize a certain one of these possibilities because he sees that this is the best on the whole. This notion of God choosing *sub ratione boni* seems to Spinoza ridiculously anthropomorphic. But it plays an essential part in Leibniz's philosophy, and in his defence of God's character. Now, of course, in Spinoza's view of God, the notion *is* ridiculous, because the whole notion of will and choice is as inapplicable to God as the notion of circularity or triangularity is to Space as a collective whole. But it does seem to me to be rather ridiculously anthropomorphic on *any* view of God. However, it is an essential feature in Leibniz's theology.

Passing now to the negative aspects of God's nature, we may remind ourselves of the following facts. God is not a monad. He has no confusion and therefore no *materia prima*. His mind perceives everything past, present, and future in the actual world, and perceives it with complete clearness. To this extent the content of God's cognition coincides with that of the humblest monad, and the only difference is that in God there is no confusion. But there is much content besides this in God's mind. In the first place, he is aware of all the details of all the possible worlds. Secondly, he is aware of all the eternal truths, which hold for all possible worlds. Thirdly, he is aware of all the facts about his own nature. Now Leibniz holds that monads below the level of rational souls cognize nothing about merely possible worlds; they also cognize no eternal truths and know nothing of God's nature. The rational souls do indeed know something of God's nature, of eternal truths, and of possible worlds. For they to some extent mirror God in addition to mirroring the rest of the created world. But presumably there is a great deal in this department which no created mind perceives even confusedly. And it is certain, in Leibniz's view, that much of the knowledge of these facts which does exist in any created mind is, and will remain in this life, confused and unconscious.

Since there is never any confusion in God's mind, and since all change is ultimately change in the distribution of confusion throughout a total field of consciousness, there can be no change in God. How Leibniz would reconcile this with the fact that God *first* contemplated all the possible worlds and *then* created the best of them, I do not know.

Again, I do not know how God could perceive the changes which take place in us, as he must do since they are real, without any change taking place in himself. But difficulties of this kind are common to all systems which make God changeless and then profess to bring him into creative and cognitive relations to a world which he originated and which has been changing ever since.

Beside having no confusion God has no point of view. According to Leibniz there is some very intimate connexion between confusion and point of view. I think he holds that any change in the distribution of confusion involves a change in point of view, and conversely. I do not think that he would deny that the total amount of confusion might vary whilst the point of view remained the same. But, however this may be, it is certain that God has no point of view. He also has no organism. This is obvious. For he perceives everything with *complete* clearness. Now the organism of a monad is a certain set of monads whose changes that monad perceives with *special* clearness. Thus God must either have no organism or must have all the created world for his organism. And Leibniz definitely rejects the notion of a World-Soul.

It is worth noting that Leibniz says in Section 14 of the *Discours* that God is aware of the actual world in two quite different ways.[1] (1) He knows it in thought as it would appear from every possible point of view, i.e. as every possible monad in it would perceive it. And (2) he knows it in a way peculiar to himself. It is this double knowledge which enables him to conceive and then create a system subject to the Pre-established harmony.

2 Existence of God

Leibniz based his belief in the existence of God on four main arguments, viz. the Ontological, the Cosmological, an argument from the Pre-established Harmony, and an argument about Eternal Truths. I will say something about each of these in turn.

2.1 Ontological Argument

Leibniz discussed this rather carefully. He accepts the main step in it without question, but he considers that a preliminary investigation is needed to decide whether the Ens Realissimum is a *possible* existent. According to him, the argument, as given by St Anselm and Descartes,

[1] [G., IV, 439. Loemker, 311–12.]

would establish only the hypothetical proposition 'If a being answering to the description of the Ens Realissimum would be a possible existent then there necessarily is a being answering to the description of the Ens Realissimum', i.e. 'if there *can* be anything answering to this description, then there *must* be something answering to it'. Now the Ens Realissimum is described as having all positive perfections to the highest degree. The preliminary question then is whether this description may not involve some internal inconsistency. If so, nothing *could* answer to it. But, if not, then something *must* answer to it, for the reasons which St Anselm and Descartes gave. Leibniz therefore sets out to prove that there can be no incompatibility between any two purely positive characteristics. This he easily does to his own satisfaction from his doctrine that all opposition is contradictory opposition, i.e. the kind of opposition which there is between *p* and non-*p*. This doctrine seems very doubtful. One does not see, e.g., how the opposition between characteristics which seem entirely positive, e.g. two colours or two different shades of the same colour, can be brought under it. But, even if it could be accepted, two difficulties would remain. (1) Of two opposed qualities, say good and evil, of which both *seem* to be positive, how could you tell which is really the purely positive one? Leibniz and most theologians who take this point of view have generally regarded the most desirable of such a pair as the positive one and the less desirable as the negative one. But, if anyone had chosen to say that evil is purely positive and good partly negative, and consequently that the Ontological Argument proves the existence of a perfectly evil being, I do not see what answer they could have given. (2) Even if the description of the Ens Realissimum involves no internal inconsistency Leibniz has done nothing to remove the fundamental objection to the Ontological Argument, viz. that it treats the existential proposition: 'The so and so exists (or is real)' as if it could be analysed in precisely the same way as the characterizing proposition 'The so and so flies (or is yellow).' In fact it seems to me that Leibniz's doctrine of the choice and creation of the best of the possible worlds rests on this fallacy. He thinks of the possible monads as already in being, and already having all their other predicates and then a certain set of them is launched on its career by being given the one remaining predicate of existence. Since creation is an unintelligible notion to us, no doubt any attempt to state what happened at creation will be nonsense. But this does seem particularly palpable nonsense.

2.2 Cosmological Argument

This is one of Leibniz's favourite arguments. Every state of the universe no doubt follows necessarily in accordance with a law from the previous state. But this previous state has as little intrinsic necessity as the one which it determines. And so on without end. So there must be one or more intrinsically necessary beings, altogether outside the course of nature; and the system of nature as a whole must depend on it or on them.

Russell makes an interesting objection to the Cosmological Argument.[1] He says that it must be formally invalid because it professes to deduce a *necessary* proposition (viz. 'There is a being who exists of necessity') from premisses which are not all necessary (e.g. 'I exist here and now'). Is there anything in this objection?

I think it is impossible to discuss it unless one states the argument formally. I think it would often be stated as follows: 'Anything which exists and whose existence is *not* necessary derives its existence from something whose existence *is* necessary. I exist and my existence is not necessary. Therefore I derive my existence from something whose existence is necessary. Therefore there is something whose existence is necessary.'

Now I do not agree that the conclusion, as stated, is a necessary proposition. It is a non-modal proposition. The conclusion is not 'There is *necessarily* something whose existence is necessary', but is simply 'There *is* something whose existence is necessary.' Nothing is asserted or implied about the modality of this proposition. So it seems to me that Russell's objection is invalid.

But there are other logical questions which could be raised about the argument. There are at least two phrases in it which are ambiguous, viz. 'necessary' and 'derives its existence from'. They might be interpreted in a purely logical sense or in a non-logical sense. I suppose that the purely logical interpretation of the statement 'The instance of ϕ necessarily exists' would be 'It is a necessary proposition that there is one and only one instance of ϕ.' I suppose that the purely logical interpretation of the statement 'The instance of ψ derives its existence from the instance of ϕ' would be 'The proposition that there is one and only one instance of ψ is entailed by the proposition that there is one and only one instance of ϕ.'

If we take these purely logical interpretations the major premiss is transformed into the following proposition: 'If it is true, but not

[1] [Russell, Section 109.]

necessary, that there is one and only one instance of any characteristic ψ, then it follows that there is a characteristic ϕ such that (1) it is necessary that there is one and only one instance of ϕ, and (2) the proposition that there is one and only one instance of ϕ entails that there is one and only one instance of ψ.'

Now it is easy to see that, if the major premiss be interpreted in this way, it is self-contradictory. For in the antecedent it is supposed that the proposition that there is one and only once instance of ψ is *not* necessary. But in the consequent it is said that the proposition that there is one and only one instance of ψ would be entailed by a proposition which *is* necessary, viz. the proposition that there is one and only one instance of ϕ. But a proposition which was entailed by a necessary proposition would itself be *necessary*. Thus the consequent in the major premiss entails the contradictory of what is supposed in the antecedent. And so the major premiss is self-contradictory.

We could, however, easily keep the purely logical interpretation and avoid the contradiction, if we were to alter the major premiss as follows. We might distinguish between being *intrinsically* necessary and being only *derivatively* necessary. An intrinsically necessary proposition would be one whose necessity arose simply from its own terms. A derivatively necessary proposition would be one whose necessity arose, not simply from its own terms, but from the fact that it is entailed by other propositions all of which are necessary. The major premiss would now take the following form: 'If it is *true* but *not intrinsically necessary* that there is one and only one instance of a characteristic ψ, then it follows that there is a characteristic ϕ such that (1) it is *intrinsically* necessary that there is one and only one instance of ϕ, and (2) the proposition that there is one and only one instance of ϕ entails the proposition that there is one and only one instance of ψ.'

There is no contradiction here. But this premiss would make *all* existential facts necessary. Those which were not intrinsically necessary would all be derivatively necessary. So this interpretation might suit Spinoza, but it would certainly not suit Leibniz or the ordinary Christian theologian. I am quite sure that they never did interpret 'deriving its existence from' in purely logical terms. They were thinking, not of logical entailment, but something analogous to the sense in which a person derives his existence from his parents, or a mental image derives its existence from a person who deliberately calls it up and keeps it before his mind's eye. The argument would then run as follows: 'Anything whose existence is causally derivative must ultimately derive it from something whose existence is not causally derivative. I exist and my existence is causally derivative. Therefore I ultimately derive my existence from something whose existence is not causally derivative. Therefore there is something whose existence is not causally derivative.'

In this argument there is no question of modality in the logical sense, and therefore not even the appearance of a modal fallacy, such as Russell suggests. Supposing that we interpret the argument in this way, there still remains the following question. Can we get beyond the partly negative conclusion that there is something whose existence is not causally derivative to the more positive conclusion that there is something whose existence is intrinsically necessary? It is certain that Leibniz and most Christian theologians have claimed to do so.

Now I think that the more positive interpretation of the conclusion could take two different forms, one purely logical and the other causal. The purely logical interpretation would be that the existence of anything whose existence is not causally derived is *logically necessary*. This would amount to saying that anything whose existence is not causally derived has a characteristic φ such that the proposition 'There is one and only one instance of φ' is logically necessary. Now Leibniz certainly held that the only entity whose existence is not causally derived has the property of possessing all positive perfections to the highest possible degree. And he held that the proposition 'There is one and only one entity which has all positive perfections to the highest possible degree' is logically necessary. Now the converse of the proposition under discussion does seem obvious. The existence of anything whose existence was logically necessary would presumably be causally underived. But I can see nothing obvious about the proposition itself. Why should there not be existents whose existence is not causally derived and also not logically necessary?

The causal way of putting a more positive interpretation on the conclusion is to pass from 'not causally deriving its existence from anything else' to 'causally deriving its existence from itself'. Theologians have often described God as *causa sui*. No doubt they often meant no more by this than that God does not causally derive his existence from anything else. But I suspect that they sometimes meant that he causally derives his existence from himself. As regards this interpretation I have two comments to make. (1) I doubt whether any clear positive idea corresponds to the phrase 'deriving one's existence from oneself'. (2) If this phrase has a clear positive meaning, I still do not see what justification there is for passing from the negative proposition 'This does not causally derive its existence from anything else' to 'This causally derives its existence from itself.' One would need the premiss 'Everything that exists causally derives its existence either from itself or from something else.' But, even if this is intelligible, is it in the least self-evident?

2.3 Argument from Pre-established Harmony

We might regard this as Leibniz's special form of the argument from ostensible teleology within nature to an architect or designer of nature. As Leibniz insists, it would be much stronger than the ordinary form of this argument. In the first place, it does not need as its premiss questionable propositions about the inner teleology of organisms or the adaptation of the rest of nature to the existence and progressive development of life and mind. The only premiss that it needs is that everything appears to interact with everything else. This seems highly plausible even on purely physical grounds, when we consider the pervasiveness of gravitation, radiation, and other physical influences. Secondly, it avoids the objection which might be made to the Cosmological Argument and the usual form of the Argument from Design, viz. that, so far as these arguments go, there might be a number of Gods. For the Pre-established harmony between causally independent substances, which is necessary to account for the appearance of universal interaction, could hardly have been arranged except by a single mind which could contemplate them all and compare all their states. Thirdly, it is often objected to the ordinary form of the Argument from Design that at best it would suggest the existence of an *Architect* of Nature of great, but not necessarily infinite, wisdom and power. Now it is plain that, if the doctrine of Pre-established Harmony be the only way to account for the appearance of universal interaction, God will have to be something much more than this. In view of the infinite number of monads in every bit of apparent matter, and in view of the fact that each monad has an organism of monads each of which has in turn an organism of monads, and so on without end, God will need infinite cognitive powers to keep his head. And in view of Leibniz's theory of substance God will have to be a creator who creates the monads at the start with such natures that they will all unfold independently and automatically in accordance with the Pre-established harmony. Of course it seems to me much more reasonable to hold that the ultimate substances in the world never have begun to exist and always have interacted with each other. But, if you deny this, Leibniz's argument for the existence of God becomes very strong. The alternative is an infinitely improbable chance correlation between the histories of an infinite number of completely independent substances.

2.4 The Argument about Eternal Truths

Leibniz's real meaning on this point is not easy to grasp. The argument will be found in Sections 43–6 inclusive of the *Monadology*.[1] I will collect his chief remarks and then try to interpret them. 'God is the source not only of existences but also of essences, so far as they are real.' He is the source 'of that which is real in the possible'. Without God 'there would be nothing real in the possible'. There would be 'not only nothing existing but also nothing possible'. The reason which Leibniz gives for these statements is that the reality of essences or possibilities or eternal truths 'must be founded on something existing and actual'. And he concludes that their reality must be founded on the existence of a being whose essence involves his existence. He then adds, by way of warning, that we must not suppose, as Descartes and others have done, that because the eternal truths are dependent on God, they are arbitrary and depend on his will. Necessary truths 'depend solely on God's understanding, and are its internal object'. Contingent truths do indeed depend on his will; but even they are not arbitrary, since the principle of God's choice is that of fitness.

These are the essential points of Leibniz's doctrine. It remains to try to interpret it. In the first place I am pretty sure that it is completely misunderstood by Russell.[2] Russell takes it to mean that the eternal truths are made true by the fact that God knows them. He has no difficulty in making nonsense of this; it is in fact plainly absurd that the truth of any proposition should consist in the fact that God or anyone else knows or believes it to be true. But, in the first place, Leibniz is hardly likely to have made such a silly mistake. And, secondly, Russell's interpretation would have no application to essences, possibilities, etc. Yet Leibniz is plainly referring just as much to them as to eternal truths. For he says that God is the source of essence as well as existence, that he is the source of the reality of the possible, and so on.

This suggests to me that what Leibniz had in mind was somewhat as follows. Possibilities that do not actually exist, essences that do not have any actual instances, and propositions which apply not only to the actual but also to the merely possible, are in some sense real. They

[1] [G., VI, 614. Loemker, 647.]   [2] [Russell, Section 112.]

have some kind of being; since they are the subjects of true propositions, and can be the objects of acts of contemplation, judgment,
etc. in existent finite minds. What kind of being can they have?
Plainly they cannot depend for their reality on either characterizing
or being contemplated by any ordinary created existent being. For, by
hypothesis, they do not characterize anything that actually exists, and
they need not be contemplated by any finite existent. Yet it seemed to
Leibniz that they could not just hang unsupported in the air; that the
being of possibilities, unexemplified characteristics, hypothetical facts,
etc., must depend in some way on something actually existent. And
his argument is that, since they must depend on *some* actual existent
and cannot depend on any finite, created, contingent existent, they
must depend on an existent whose existence is entailed by its essence.
Thus his doctrine comes to this: There must be an essence which
entails the existence of an actual instance of itself. Let us call this 'The
Supreme Essence' and let us call its instance 'The Intrinsically Necessary Existent'. The being of all other essences depends on the existence
of the Intrinsically Necessary Existent. The fact that certain of these
other essences are exemplified in finite created existents, and that the
rest of them are not, depends on the *will* of the Intrinsically Necessary
Existent. Leibniz is commonly said to have held that the possible is
logically prior to the actually existent; and he has often been criticized
on this ground. If my interpretation of his Argument about Eternal
Truths be right, his doctrine about the relations of the possible and the
actually existent is not nearly so simple as this. The actually existent
must first be divided into the created and the uncreated. These divisions
are exhaustive and exclusive. The possible is logically prior to the *created*
existent, in the sense that the latter is the actualization of one out of a
number of alternative possibilities all of which are equally real. But the
possible is not logically prior to the *uncreated* existent; for the being of
all these unactualized possibilities depends on the existence of the latter.

If this be Leibniz's doctrine it is at least not open to the charge of
being simply silly, as it would be on Russell's interpretation of it. The
question of what kind of being should be ascribed to mere possibilities
and to purely hypothetical facts is a real problem, and Leibniz's theory
of God as the existent from which all possibilities derive their being is
one attempt to solve it. But, when he goes into details, he does lay
himself open to the kind of charge that Russell makes. The possible
worlds and the eternal truths may, in some way which we cannot
understand, depend on God's existence for their being. And they
would, no doubt, also be contents of God's intellect, in the sense that

he would contemplate the possibilities and would know the eternal truths. But the former fact cannot possibly be reduced to, or explained in terms of, the latter.

3 Defence of God's character

Leibniz wrote the *Theodicy* mainly to show that the evil in the world is compatible with its having been created by a perfectly good and wise being. We had better begin with Leibniz's doctrine of evil. He distinguishes three kinds of evil, which he calls *metaphysical, moral,* and *physical*. Moral evil is sin, and physical evil is pain. Metaphysical evil is limitation. Every monad necessarily has it, for it is identical with *materia prima*. God, having every positive characteristic to the highest possible degree, has no metaphysical evil in him. Now Leibniz always maintained that metaphysical evil is purely negative or primitive; it is simply the extent to which each monad falls short of God. One consequence of this should be that every finite mind is infinitely evil; but perhaps a good many theologians would not object to this. Now metaphysical evil is supposed to be fundamental, and physical and moral evil are supposed to be dependent on it. Leibniz concluded that sin and pain must be purely negative, since they are due to metaphysical evil, and this is purely negative.

We may as well criticize this theory at once. (1) There is a certain ambiguity in the word 'evil', since it may be used as a substantive, as when we say that toothache is an evil, or as an adjective, viz. the ethical characteristic common and peculiar to evils. Now the doctrine of the negativity of evil might mean that the characteristic 'evilness' is purely negative, like blindness, i.e. that it is just non-goodness. Or it might mean that, whilst 'evilness' is a positive characteristic, it attaches to things only in virtue of what they lack and not in virtue of anything positive in them. Thus 'hungriness' is a positive characteristic, but it attaches to a person simply because he lacks food. Of these two alternatives I should say that both are false, and that the first is ridiculous. But Leibniz is forced to take the first and more ridiculous form of the theory for the following reason. Goodness and evilness are opposites, and on his view all opposition reduces to contradictory opposition. Now he wants to hold that God is perfectly good and not perfectly evil, and that all God's attributes are purely positive. But, if goodness be purely positive, and all opposition is to be contradictory opposition, evilness must simply be non-goodness. (2) It is plainly false that painfulness is negative or that all pains are simply the absence of something positive. And it is very awkward for a Christian to maintain that sinfulness or sins are purely negative. Indeed a good many theologians have been in the unhappy position of wanting sin to be negative in order that God may not be blamed for creating sinners, and wanting it to be positive in order that he may be justified in damning them. (3) Even if metaphysical evil be purely negative, and if it be a necessary condition of physical and moral evil, it does not follow that these consequences of it will be purely negative. (4) Leibniz does not explain in detail how mere internal limitation gives rise to sin, and still less does he explain how it gives rise to pain. (5) It is quite clear that *materia prima* must be more than mere lack of something positive if it is to do all the work which Leibniz demands of it in his physics, metaphysics, and theory of knowledge.

Now it is metaphysically necessary that any created universe should contain some metaphysical evil. For any possible created universe must consist of monads, and any monad must have some degree of confusion, i.e. some amount of *materia prima*, and therefore some amount of metaphysical evil. It would also be necessary that any universe which contained more than one monad should have the total metaphysical evil in it unequally distributed. For two monads in the same universe must necessarily differ in degree of confusion and therefore in amount of metaphysical evil. Leibniz seems to think it obvious that, since every possible world must contain some metaphysical evil, every possible world must contain some sin and some pain. This, however, does not seem to follow from the mere fact that sin and pain are due to metaphysical evil. For it seems possible that there should be a great deal of metaphysical evil and no moral or physical evil. Suppose, e.g., that the world had consisted only of bare monads, and had contained no animal souls and no rational souls. Then there would have been a great deal of metaphysical evil, since all these monads would have been highly confused and bursting with *materia prima*. But there would certainly have been no sin. And I do not think that Leibniz could hold that there would have been any pain. For he distinctly says that pleasure and pain are due to *noticeable* furtherings or checkings of appetition. And this implies that they could not exist in a being which had no clear consciousness. So it seems to me that God would not have the simple choice of deciding to create the world with the least possible amount of metaphysical evil. He might have to balance the three kinds of evil against each other, even though the other two would not be there unless there were metaphysical evil. However, Leibniz does not consider these complications.

The situation before God is therefore the following. It is logically impossible for him to create a world without metaphysical evil in it. And he cannot do what is logically impossible. Now God is perfectly good. For Leibniz has assumed that, of the two opposites good and evil, good is the positive one; and God is the being who has all positive characteristics to the highest degree. Again, God cannot choose capriciously. It is a necessary truth that there must be a sufficient reason for anything that actually takes place; and so there must be a sufficient reason for God's decision to create rather than to abstain from creating, and there must be a sufficient reason for God's decision to create this world rather than any of the other possible worlds. Now, for a perfectly good and wise being who has two alternatives A and B open to him the only possible sufficient reason for preferring A to B would be the superior goodness on the whole of A to B. This consideration is necessary and sufficient to determine the choice of such a being. The doctrine of the purely negative nature of evil comes in over the question Why did God decide to create rather than not to create, seeing that there is necessarily some evil in every possible universe? If evil be something positive we should have to show that in one at least of the possible universes there is a balance of good over evil. It is very difficult to see how this could be shown. But with Leibniz's view of evil it is not necessary to show this. Any universe would be better than none. For it would have something positive in it and this would be good, whilst the evil in it would only be what it lacked. There can be no question of a balance between something positive and a mere negation. The fact that we all do consider that good and evil balance against each other, and that the mere absence of any universe would not be a positive evil but merely an absence of *both good and evil*, shows that Leibniz's doctrine is at variance with the facts. And of course he does not consistently keep to anything so absurd. But it is his only ground for showing that God, who could have abstained from creating, acted rightly in creating rather than abstaining.

Granted that *any* universe is better than none at all, God has now only to decide *which one* he will create. And here his decision is determined simply by the relative amounts of metaphysical perfection in each. It is plain that the doctrine comes in the end to this, that God will create as much as is logically possible for him to create. In this, I suppose, intensity and degree will have to be counted as well as mere number of substances and states. Everything positive is wholly good; and the more there is of it, and the greater the intensity of anything that has intensive magnitude, the more goodness there will be. Now, if one tries to think this out, it becomes very difficult to see how God is limited at all. We are explicitly told that he is limited only by the laws of logic and pure mathematics. He is not subject to physical necessity, i.e. he is not faced with an alien and independent material with laws and properties of its own. Nor is there any question of having a limited space or duration or amount of material at his disposal. Lastly, we are explicitly told that, in the end, all opposition is purely contradictory opposition, i.e. the sort of opposition which there is between the presence and the absence of something. If so, surely all that is positive in each of the possible worlds must be compossible. The incompossibility between two possible worlds W_1 and W_2 can consist only in the fact that some positive factor F is present in W_1 and absent in W_2 or present in W_2 and absent in W_1. Since there can be no incompatibility between the positive features in W_1 and W_2 God *can* create at once all that is positive in both. He *ought* to do so, if all that is positive is wholly good. And, as a perfectly good being who is morally necessitated to do the best that is open to him, he is morally necessitated to do this. Thus, in the end, Leibniz ought to come to the same conclusion as Spinoza, viz. that all that is possible is actual. Moreover, there can be no possible reason why God should have put off creating the best possible world; for any delay in creating it means so much less positive existence, and therefore on Leibniz's view, so much less goodness and more evil. It would therefore seem that God cannot have existed before he created the world, and so the world must be co-eternal with him. So it seems to me that, if Leibniz had consistently developed this side of his system, he would have reached a result which would hardly differ from Spinozism so far as concerns the relations of God and the world.

It will be noticed that Leibniz's Optimism, of which so much fun has been made by Voltaire and others, comes to very little. No doubt Leibniz said that this is the best of all possible worlds, and no doubt this sounds fatuously optimistic in view of the enormous amount of moral and physical evil which it contains. But, quite apart from the doctrine of the negativity of evil, it is compatible with this world being extremely bad and even containing a balance of evil. For it merely asserts that any other possible world would have contained a greater balance of evil. The fact is that Leibniz was much more concerned to save God's character than to take an optimistic view of the actual world. So long as the actual world contained the slightest positive balance of good over evil, and so long as it could be shown to be logically impossible that any alternative world would have contained a greater balance, God's character is saved. And this was all that Leibniz cared about.

Can anything be made of such a theory as Leibniz's? (1) In the first place, we should have to drop the doctrine that the characteristic of evilness is negative, that it is merely the absence of goodness. We might, however, try to keep the doctrine that, although evilness is a positive characteristic, yet evils are all negative. The only form in which this could possibly be maintained is, I think, the following. It would have to mean that a thing or event has the positive ethical characteristic of evilness only in virtue of its negative non-ethical characteristics, i.e. because of what it is not and not because of anything that it is. Even this is plainly unsatisfactory. Both a stone and a selfish man lack love of their neighbours. We call the man evil in virtue of this negative characteristic, but we do not call the stone evil. Thus, even if a negative non-ethical characteristic be necessary, it is never sufficient, to give a thing the ethical characteristic of evilness. At the very most we can say that a thing is never evil on account of its positive non-ethical qualities alone; it is always the combination of certain negative non-ethical characteristics with certain positive ones which makes it evil. Thus the only form of the doctrine of the negativity of evil which could possibly be maintained is this: 'Evilness is as positive an ethical characteristic as goodness; and a thing must exist, and have certain positive non-ethical characteristics, in order to be evil, just as much as in order to be good. But it is never evil merely in respect of its positive non-ethical characteristics. Its evilness is always due to the combination of certain negative non-ethical characteristics with its positive non-ethical characteristics. On the other hand, if a thing is good, it is so in virtue of its purely positive non-ethical characteristics. It is never good in virtue of what it lacks.' It must be noted that, on this view, a universe might quite well contain a balance of evil. For it might not be particularly good in virtue of its purely positive non-ethical characteristics, and it might be very evil in virtue of the combination of what it lacks with what it has. Thus a sane interpretation of the negativity of evil gives no countenance to the view that *any* universe is better than no universe at all. No universe at all means no value and no disvalue. And, as we have just seen, a universe may have a balance of evil.

(2) Could Leibniz have dropped the negativity of evil and still have defended God's character? Leibniz's defence of God's wisdom and goodness is to limit his power. But he wants to limit it *only* to the extent that God cannot perform logical and metaphysical impossibilities.

And he wants God to be a creator and not a mere architect, and to have created of deliberate choice and not from metaphysical necessity. Now it is of course easy to save God's goodness and wisdom, without assuming that evil is in any sense negative, provided you are willing to limit his power enough. If you will admit that he did not create his materials, but was faced with independent materials with laws and properties of their own, you can always say that he did his best and that Gods can do no more. But this of course makes God a mere architect, and makes him limited by physical as well as logical or metaphysical necessity. Again, if you suppose that God could not help creating what he did create, you can save his wisdom and goodness without limiting his power further and without needing to assume that evil is in any sense negative. But this would have removed almost the last trace of difference between Leibniz's God and Spinoza's. I am inclined to think that the doctrine of the negativity of evil was essential if Leibniz was to defend the character of a deliberately creative God whose power is limited only by logical and metaphysical necessity. For he had to show that any created universe was better than none at all, and that it is *logically* impossible that any created universe should have been better than the actual one. And I do not see how he could hope to have proved either proposition without his own special form of the doctrine of the negativity of evil. Since the doctrine, in the form in which he has to hold it, is plainly ridiculous, he succeeds neither in defending God's character nor in showing that the actual universe does not contain a balance of evil.

(3) Before leaving the subject there is one other point worth mentioning. In comparing possible worlds it would be necessary to distinguish the total value *in* a world and the total value *of* a world. The former would consist in the virtue, happiness, etc. of each individual. The latter would consist in the value of the society formed by these individuals. The value of a society would of course depend in part on the values in it; but it would also depend to a large extent on the relations of the individuals to each other and to God. Since Leibniz denies the reality of relations he might have argued that there is no value *of* a universe as distinct from the value *in* it. But, when he is discussing ethics and theology, he forgets about the denial of relations. And there are passages in which he does take the line that a whole may be perfect though the parts are not. This plainly does introduce the notion of the value *of* a whole as distinct from the value *in* it. And, however inconsistent it may be with his denial of relations, he explicitly says that the rational souls in the universe form a spiritual

community with God as their king. This is the origin of Kant's conception of the Kingdom of Ends. I will conclude by saying something about this.

4 The Kingdom of Ends

Leibniz always made it a great merit of his philosophy that it reconciled teleology and final causation, on the one hand, with mechanism and efficient causation, on the other. The situation on this subject at his time was roughly as follows. The Scholastics had made great use of the concepts of end and of final causation. With Descartes they have been almost completely pushed out of the created world. Within the world they have no place except in the voluntary action of human beings. Everything else is to be explained mechanically, and it remains extremely paradoxical that human minds can interfere with this universal mechanism even to the extent of initiating bodily movements by their volitions. But God does act from final causes. He creates and arranges matter and the laws of matter in such a way that his designs shall be carried out by purely mechanical processes. Spinoza eliminated final causation both from the finite individual and from God. The finite modes have will, but they are not really moved by desires for ends. They are simply pushed by impulses, which create the illusion that ends are being desired. And to ascribe will and designs to God is as absurd as to ascribe figure and motion to him. Now Leibniz saw clearly that scientific explanation of natural phenomena had to be by mechanism and efficient causation, and that there was no hope of going back to Scholasticism on this point. On the other hand, it seemed clear to him that there was final causation both *within* the universe and *of* the universe. And he claimed that his theory of monads did justice to both these facts.

According to Leibniz there are two harmonies within the world, viz. a harmony between efficient and final causation, and a harmony between the kingdom of nature and the kingdom of grace. Both these harmonies are ultimately due to the fundamental Pre-established harmony between all the monads and to God's choice of the best of all possible worlds.

4.1 Efficient and final causation

The harmony between efficient and final causation is most fully stated in the *Monadology*, sections 78–81.[1] The empirical facts with which Leibniz is here concerned are those which have led people to deny the possibility of interaction between the human soul and the human body. The facts are that the human body seems to be a physical system subject to the general principles of mechanics such as the conservation of energy and momentum. Descartes had held that this excludes all action of the mind on the body except that it can change the direction of the flow of animal spirits in the brain by moving the pineal gland in various directions. Leibniz argued that even this would be impossible because, although such action would be compatible with the conservation of *vis viva*, it would not be compatible with the conservation of *angular momentum*. Yet of course the soul seems to move certain parts of the body at will. Leibniz sums up the situation by saying that 'bodies act as if (which is impossible) there were no souls, souls act as if there were no bodies, and both act as if they influenced each other'. He also says that 'souls act according to the laws of final causes, by appetitions, ends, and means. Bodies act in accordance with the laws of efficient causes or of motion. And the two realms, that of efficient causes and that of final causes, are in harmony with each other.'

Now I think that his reconciliation of efficient and final causation may be stated as follows. Strictly speaking, all causation is final, i.e. all causes are of the nature of desire or impulse and all effects are processes which are started by desire or impulse and which tend to bring about its satisfaction. What appears as a bit of matter, whether it be a human body or anything else, is a set of very confused minds. And what appear as changes in a bit of matter are changes which these minds produce in themselves by impulses and desires. Now all these changes in the lower monads are subject to certain general limiting conditions. Since the changes are really psychical these general limiting conditions must really be psychological laws about the mental processes which are initiated by unsatisfied desire and which tend to satisfy the desire. But, since the changes are misperceived as motions of matter under the action of external forces, these psychological laws will appear to us as the general laws of motion. Now these laws are contingent. They hold in the actual world, but different laws might have held. And at this point the notion of final cause enters again in another way. Since the laws might have been different, their actual form must be due to the fact that God saw that a world in which these laws held would be on the whole better than a world in which any other laws had held. Leibniz thought that the fact that the actual laws can be expressed in

[1] [G., VI, 620–1. Loemker, 651.]

terms of principles of conservation and of minimum principles was a sign that they result from the volitions of a good and wise being and are not metaphysically necessary. Leibniz never tells us what the psychological laws are which appear to us as such principles as the conservation of energy and of momentum. And, granted that a good and wise being would choose laws which take the form of conservation-principles and minimum-principles, it is not obvious why he should decide that *momentum* and *energy* should be conserved rather than the other physical magnitudes which are not conserved.

The position then is this. Strictly speaking, all action is by final causes, and the laws which govern it are psychological laws. But only the higher monads, viz. animal souls and rational spirits, appear to us to act from final causes. The lower monads, or rather certain groups of them, appear as matter; their changes appear as the movements of matter determined by efficient causation; and the laws which govern these changes appear as the laws of motion. Yet, even when we see the laws in this partly distorted form we can see that they are the *results of* final causation by God, though we cannot see that they are *laws about* final causation in created substances. For their form irresistibly suggests that they are not metaphysically necessary, but result from the deliberate choice of a wise and good being. Now this being, when he created the monads, adjusted the states of all of them to each other. When the soul of a given organism explicitly desires an end and takes means to attain it, the whole causal process is really in itself. But the monads in its organism will meanwhile go through a parallel series of changes, which will appear as the appropriate movements of limbs, etc. And all these changes will be subject to those general laws which, when stated in phenomenal terms, are the laws of motion. To us it appears that the process starts with a desire in the soul, that this affects the body and sets up changes in the outer world, and that finally these affect the soul and produce changes which satisfy the desire. (Cf., e.g., the case of a man designing a house and getting it built.) But this is a delusion. There is one process of change which is wholly in the soul, and which starts with the desire and ends with the satisfaction. Parallel with this there is a process of change in the monads of the organism, and in other monads. And this appears as appropriate movements of the organism and of foreign bodies, subject to the laws of motion. That these two independent series agree in the way in which they do is due to the particular arrangements which God made when he originally established the harmony between all the monads at creation. The theory may be illustrated by the following diagram, where crosses represent events in a ruling monad, and noughts represent events in those monads which are misperceived as its body and as foreign matter. The full arrows represent the real causal relation, and the dotted arrows represent the apparent causal relation. Leibniz's doctrine, that what appears to us as mechanical and physical laws are really psycho-

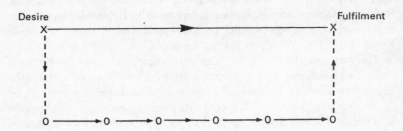

logical laws of minds of a very low order which are slaves of habit and association, is taken up and worked out more fully by Ward, in his *Pluralism and Theism.*[1] Ward makes it more plausible by the following consideration. Even if we take the ordinary scientific view of atoms and molecules as being entirely non-mental, we must admit that the laws of physics and mechanics are not laws about individual atoms and molecules. The smallest bit of matter that we could possibly perceive and experiment with is a collection of many millions of atoms and molecules. Consequently the laws of physics and mechanics must, on any view, be regarded as statements about statistical averages. If, then, the atoms and molecules be really mental substances, the laws of physics and mechanics must be compared, not with the psychological laws which govern individual minds, but with statistical laws about large collections of minds. The conservation of energy, e.g., is comparable to the fact that the proportion of the inhabitants of England who marry or commit suicide in each year is practically constant. We know that individuals have the most varied motives for marrying and committing suicide, and yet this fact is compatible with the proportion of marriages and suicides for any large community keeping practically constant. If this be so with communities of minds at the human level, it is *a fortiori* likely that collections of minds at the level of bare monads would exhibit statistical uniformities. There is nothing in this argument which Leibniz could not have accepted, and it certainly very much strengthens his case. Monism about differentiating attributes, if it can be made to work, is certainly more satisfactory to the intellect than

[1] [James Ward, *The Realm of Ends: or Pluralism and Theism* (Cambridge, 1911).]

dualism or pluralism. And a mentalistic type of monism about differentiating attributes is certainly more satisfactory than a materialistic type, provided it will give a plausible explanation of the laws of mechanics and physics. For it seems quite impossible to explain the higher types of mental fact materialistically, whilst it does not seem impossible to regard physical and chemical laws as statistical uniformities about very large collections of very stupid minds. Now it does seem impossible to regard minds as mere occurrents in a single continuant; and so, if we adopt mentalistic monism about differentiating attributes, we are almost forced to adopt substantial pluralism. Thus a combination of a mentalistic monism about attributes with pluralism about substances is perhaps the most plausible form for a system of speculative philosophy to take, if it is to be intelligible and to do justice to all known aspects of the universe. It does not of course follow, nor is it very likely, that it is the whole truth and nothing but the truth; but it may well be the best approximation to the truth that human beings in their present life can reach. We must remember the extremely narrow basis from which all attempts at speculative philosophy by human beings must start. We can describe and interpret the world intelligibly to ourselves only in terms of what we are directly acquainted with. Now each of us is directly acquainted with two and only two things, viz. (1) his sense-fields and the relations and changes of relation among the sensa in these fields, and (2) his own mind, its experiences and activities, and the relations and changes of relation between these. Any theory of the universe which we can either make or understand must describe the universe by analogy with one or other or a mixture of these two objects of direct acquaintance. This is a beggarly equipment for so vast an undertaking, and this fact makes it unreasonable to attach much weight to any system of speculative philosophy. But no human being can step outside these limitations, and the desire to form a coherent theory of the universe seems to be innate in human beings. We must therefore judge systems of speculative philosophy by what they accomplish with the available materials, and not by some super-human standard which is no more attainable by the critics than by the author. And, within these limits, a system like Leibniz's must be given a very high place.

4.2 Nature and grace

We come now to the second harmony within the universe, viz. the harmony between the realm of nature and the realm of grace. The realm of nature consists of the non-rational monads, i.e. the bare monads which appear to us as matter and the animal souls. The realm of grace consists of rational monads and God. It thus includes human spirits and any rational created beings above the human level, e.g. angels and devils. Owing to the fact that the rational spirits to some extent mirror God and have conscious desires and can act on principles, they form a society, whilst the other monads do not. God stands in the relation of creator and architect to the whole created world, but he stands in an additional relation to the realm of rational spirits, viz. that of a governor. The spirits can to some extent understand the nature and purposes of God. They know that he exists, that he is perfectly good and wise, and that they ought to obey him. And they can either deliberately try to obey him and carry out his designs or they can deliberately set themselves in opposition to him. They can therefore be justly rewarded or punished by him. Now Leibniz holds that the rewarding of good spirits and the punishment of bad spirits is not accomplished by special miraculous interventions which God makes from time to time. God foresaw all the good actions and all the bad actions which spirits would perform in the whole course of history when he created them. And he so arranged the monads which appear as matter that the spirits would automatically be punished or rewarded at the right time by the ordinary laws of nature. E.g. the monads which appear as matter were so designed and arranged by God at their creation that their own internal development would have reached the stage which appeared as the Flood by the time that human spirits had reached the degree of wickedness that justified a universal deluge as a punishment. This is what Leibniz means by the harmony between the realm of nature and the realm of grace.

The following comments may be made on this theory. (1) The conception of a community of spirits with God as their king seems meaningless unless there be real relations both between one spirit and another and between the spirits and God. (2) Since there are no causal relations between different substances the reward of the good and the punishment of the wicked by events in the material world must be an illusion. No one can really have been drowned by the Flood. The wicked at that time had a characteristic kind of painful experience which they mistakenly attributed to the action of water on their bodies. But really in each of them the painful experience must have been completely caused by his own previous mental states, conscious and unconscious. The fact that the monads which appear as matter had then reached the stage of development which appeared as the Flood was causally quite irrelevant. (3) This raises the general question: Why did God create non-rational monads at all? The ordinary theist can say that, although matter has no intrinsic value, yet it has an instrumental value. It supplies rational spirits with pleasures and pains, and with a field for their inventive, constructive, and artistic activities. And these have intrinsic value. But Leibniz cannot consistently take this view. For the monads which, when suitably grouped together, appear to rational souls as matter can neither act upon nor be acted upon by rational souls. They have therefore neither intrinsic nor instrumental value, and it is difficult to see why God should have created them. To this Leibniz would certainly have answered that mere quantity of existence is a metaphysical good. And he would have said that the infinite complexity of the realm of nature is valuable as manifesting the infinite power and wisdom of God even though it does not otherwise affect created spirits for good or ill.

Could he have gone further than this? Not, I think, so long as he held the theory of representative perception. According to that theory God could have given to any monad all those perceptions which in fact correspond to other monads and their states, even though he had created no other monad but it. So whatever value may accrue to a monad through the internal complexity and arrangement of its experiences could have arisen even though it had been the only monad that was ever created. But I have said earlier that it seems to me that Leibniz *could* consistently have held a theory of *direct* perception, though I am practically certain that he did not in fact do so. Now, on that view of perception, there would have been an additional reason for creating those monads which, when suitably grouped, are misperceived by us as bits of matter. For, if the theory of direct perception were true, each monad would be directly, but confusedly and in many cases unconsciously, acquainted with every other monad. Its sense-field at any moment would actually *consist of* all the other monads; it would not consist of states of itself representative of all the other monads. Therefore, on this view, it would be impossible for the experience of a monad to have the complexity and richness which it does have unless the other monads, which are the immediate objects of its perceptions, existed for it to perceive. On this view it would still be the case that the monads which, when grouped in certain ways, are perceived as matter do not affect spirits *causally* for good or ill. But, unless they had existed for spirits to perceive, the experiences of spirits would have been infinitely poorer in content and complexity. On these lines I think that Leibniz could have explained, consistently with his doctrine that no monad can causally influence any other, why God should have created the monads which appear as matter. And I cannot think of any other way in which he could have done so. But in fact that line of explanation is not open to him, because it seems quite certain that he held the theory of representative perception and not the theory of direct acquaintance of one monad with others.

BIBLIOGRAPHICAL NOTE

In his list of Leibniz's principal philosophical works Broad refers to editions which are not easily accessible. The reader may therefore find it helpful to have a list of those works in the more widely available C. I. Gerhardt's *Die Philosophischen Schriften von G. W. Leibniz*, vols. I–VII (Berlin, 1875–90).

In the following list I also give, in each case, a currently available English translation. With the exception of *Theodicy* I always refer to L. E. Loemker's *G. W. Leibniz: Philosophical Papers and Letters* (2nd ed., Dordrecht, 1969); but in a few cases I also mention other translations.

1 *Discours de métaphysique.* G., IV, 427–63. Loemker, 303–30.

   Mention should also be made of the following important edition. *Leibniz: Discours de métaphysique*, édition collationnée avec le texte autographe présentée et annotée par Henri Lestienne (Paris, 1907; reprinted 1929). An English translation based mainly on this edition is *Leibniz: Discourse on Metaphysics*, trans. by Peter G. Lucas and Leslie Grint (Manchester, 1953). Loemker's translation is based mainly on Gerhardt, but takes account of the edition by Lestienne.

2 *Correspondence with Arnauld.* G., II, 11–138.

   The Leibniz–Arnuald Correspondence, ed. and trans. by H. T. Mason (Manchester, 1967). Selections in Loemker, 331–50, 359–62.

3 *The New System.* G., IV, 477–87. Loemker, 453–9.

   Loemker's translation is of the original text as printed in the *Journal des Savants*, 27 June 1695, and reproduced in *G. W. Leibniz: Ausgewählte Philosophische Schriften im Originaltext*, herausgegeben von Herman Schmalenbach, vol. I (Leipzig, 1914), 119–31. Gerhardt gives a later version.

4 *Controversy with Pierre Bayle.* G., IV, 517–71.

   Selections in Loemker, 492–7, 574–85.

5 *Letters to John Bernoulli.* These are lacking in G., but are included in G. M., III, 113–973.

   Selections in Loemker, 515–41.

6 *Letters to de Volder.* G., II, 153–283.

   Selections in Loemker, 515–41.

7 *Letters to des Bosses.* G., II, 291–521.
   Selections in Loemker, 596–617.
8 *Theodicy.* G., VI, 21–463.
   Theodicy: Essays on the Goodness of God, the Freedom of Man and the Origin of Evil by G. W. Leibniz, trans. by E. M. Huggard (London, 1952).
9 *Principles of Nature and of Grace.* G., VI, 598–606.
   Loemker, 636–42.
10 *Monadology.* G., VI, 607–23.
   Loemker, 643–53.
11 *Correspondence with Clarke.* G., VII, 352–440.
   The Leibniz–Clarke Correspondence, ed. by H. G. Alexander (Manchester, 1956). Loemker, 675–721. Loemker omits Clarke's Fifth Reply.

INDEX OF PROPER NAMES